A GÜNTER GRASS SYMPOSIUM

A Günter Grass Symposium

Edited by A. LESLIE WILLSON

PUBLISHED FOR THE DEPARTMENT
OF GERMANIC LANGUAGES

THE UNIVERSITY OF TEXAS AT AUSTIN
BY THE UNIVERSITY OF TEXAS PRESS,
AUSTIN AND LONDON

International Standard Book Number 0–292–70121–7

Library of Congress Catalog Card Number 77–175531

© 1971 by *Dimension*/ The Department of Germanic Languages

ACKNOWLEDGMENTS

Permission to quote from the novels and poems is due to the kindness of the Hermann Luchterhand Verlag in Neuwied am Rhein and to Mrs. Helen Wolff, for Helen and Kurt Wolff Books, Harcourt Brace Jovanovich, New York.

The drawing by Günter Grass is taken from his pamphlet essay, *Die Ballerina*, 2d. ed. 1965 in the Friedenauer Presse, Berlin. © 1963 by Günter Grass.

CONTENTS

Preface   vii

Perspective: The Dance of Art   A. LESLIE WILLSON   3

Günter Grass   ANDRZEJ WIRTH   18
and the Dilemma of Documentary Drama

The Dogmatism of Pain: ERHARD FRIEDRICHSMEYER   32
Local Anaesthetic

The Poet's Dilemma: RALPH FREEDMAN   46
The Narrative Worlds of Günter Grass

Grass and the Denial of Drama   W. G. CUNLIFFE   60

Moralist and Jester: MICHAEL HAMBURGER   71
The Poetry of Günter Grass

A Short Bibliography of Günter Grass and   87
Works in English Translations

Authors and Translators   88

Index of Names and Titles   91

PREFACE

The Eleventh Annual Symposium sponsored by the Department of Germanic Languages at The University of Texas at Austin concentrated on the works of Günter Grass, the most electrifying and revolutionary German writer of the age. Five diverse men—literary and dramatic critics, scholars, translators—have contributed their views in five essays on the drama, prose, and poetry of Grass. The editor of the volume offers, instead of an introduction, an essay that seeks to orient the reader to the aesthetics of Günter Grass.

The Symposium was held in Austin, Texas, on April 5–8, 1970. Coincidental with the Symposium lectures, the Department of Drama presented the English premiere of *Uptight,* the editor's translation of Grass's most recent play, *Davor.*

The Symposium lectures first appeared in a special issue of *Dimension,* along with four scenes from the play.

Austin, Texas   A. Leslie Willson

A GÜNTER GRASS SYMPOSIUM

THE DANCE OF ART

A. LESLIE WILLSON

Up to now I have written poems, plays, and prose; all three types of writing are, in my case, based on dialogue, even the poetry. And so the transition from poetry to drama happened like this: poems were written in dialogue form, and were then extended. That was shortly after the war. Then slowly, gradually, stage directions were added, and so, parallel with my main occupation at that time, sculpture, I evolved my first play. That is why in a relatively short time, between 1954 and 1957, I wrote four full-length and two one-act plays, which, just like my poems and my prose, contain fantastic and realistic elements; these fantastic and realistic elements rub against each other and keep each other in check.

—Günter Grass[1]

STRESS AND COUNTER-STRESS, TENSION AND COUNTER-TENSION IN ACCORD-ance with immutable laws of physics produce balance—a virtuous condition in the natural world, often enough short-lived but ever necessarily reasserting itself. In the realm of the plastic arts the same law holds, both in regard to material masses—else the statue would tip over and smash—and in regard to another phenomenon of physics, light, thus in the play of darkness and brightness through planes of shadow and highlight. Graphic arts operate under the same rule when color counters color and perspective meets perspective, contrasting, exacting definition. Dialogue—voice against voice, word jousting with word, idea clashing with idea—ends with the keystone of compromise, furnishing at least momentary stability. In the grandest dimension cosmic chaos is content seeking the divinely imposed discipline of form—from the tumultuous encounter balance results and worlds evolve.

1. Günter Grass, *Four Plays* (New York: A Helen and Kurt Wolff Book, Harcourt, Brace & World, 1967), quoted in the introductory remarks by Martin Esslin, pp. viii–ix. The remark is quoted in German by Kurt Lothar Tank in *Günter Grass* (Berlin: Colloquium Verlag, 1965), p. 37.

This immense process has its counterpart in the microcosm of the human dimension.

In his Princeton lecture of 1966 Günter Grass states that a poem knows no compromise, but that human beings live by compromise. He implies that the poem is a thing complete, form and content in balance, and thus *is* compromise. But he continues: Whoever actively endures the tension of compromise is a fool and affects the world.[2] The fool, the jester, the clown structures his world through his own mental or physical exertions—through wit and acrobatics—and is the creator of something harmonious, is an artist. The poet and writer is such an artist, who through the exertion of his own disciplined talent balances the scale between form and content, mediates the mistrustful encounter, and evolves a work of art.

Content is counter-form; it resists form. Content and form are naturally mistrustful of one another. A work of art is produced when the hand of the artist, challenged by the resistance of content to form, brings them together in a harmonious balance. In his essay "Content as Resistance" Grass discusses the aesthetics of this artistic process metaphorically and illustrates it with an exemplary confrontation: in a dialogue. At the outset he states his intention of strewing mistrust between punctuation marks, his way of saying that the punctuation of his sentences will encompass provocation to mistrust. Indeed, he continues, his intention is to sow mistrust between form and content.[3] Content is the unavoidable factor of resistance, unprotean, resistance which provokes structural action on the part of the writer. The character of genuine content is "ghostly, snail-like, sensitive, minute in detail, difficult to locate and to hold, although it lies on the street often and acts natural" (57). Contents (a plural thing for Grass) "wear themselves out, disguise themselves, pretend to be stupid, call themselves banal, hoping thereby to escape the painful manipulation of the hand of the artist" (57), who with craft and intuition seeks out the proper form for them. In fact, contents lie in plain sight on the street, disgusted with themselves, and ashamed of their content-natures (57). They are unfulfilled, afraid of fulfillment, timid and tremulous at the approach of the artist's hand, proffering form.

2. The concluding remark of "Vom mangelnden Selbstvertrauen der schreibenden Hofnarren unter Berücksichtigung nicht vorhandener Höfe," in Günter Grass, *Über das Selbstverständliche* (Neuwied: Luchterhand, 1968), p. 112; the essay is in English translation by Ralph Manheim in Günter Grass, *Speak Out!* (New York: A Helen and Kurt Wolff Book, Harcourt, Brace & World, 1969), pp. 47–53.

3. Günter Grass, "Der Inhalt als Widerstand," in *Über meinen Lehrer Döblin und andere Vorträge* (Berlin: Literarisches Colloquium, 1968), p. 56. Further references to the essay are indicated by page numbers parenthetically in the text.

The metaphor of the shy and reluctant, resistant content (an object often enough) and its susceptibility to the imposition of false form (of which it is naturally enough mistrustful) is expanded by Grass in a dialogue between two poets, Pempelfort and Krudewil. On a sylvan stroll the Romanticist Pempelfort picks metaphorical flowers (all flowers are metaphors to him), and the Realist Krudewil pokes his stout hardwood cane into molehills. It turns out that Pempelfort habitually conjures up his Muse by overindulgence in spiced and indigestion-inducing foods which produce fitful sleep and dark dreams from which he awakens poetically inspired, sharp pencil at hand. As ghastly as this process of poetic inspiration may seem, Krudewil's practice is just as suspect. His own method of conjuring up a poem is to turn the light on and off three times, to disarm miracle. But with handy yarn he engages Pempelfort in the knitting of a new Muse. The new Muse, a proper housewife, is to be gray, mistrustful, and devoid of any knowledge of botany, of the heavens, and of death—three staples of traditional content.

In his book *Günter Grass* Kurt Lothar Tank considers the aesthetic burden of "Content as Resistance" to be paraphrased in the one-act play *Only Ten Minutes to Buffalo*.[4] It is true that there is a broad hint in the reappearance in the play of the two fussing poets Pempelfort and Krudewil. However, no longer in bardic guise, they play other roles. Having abandoned games with a bossy female playmate, Fregatte, they now romp on an abandoned steam locomotive in a green, cow-strewn (and cowchip-strewn) meadow until the appearance of Fregatte transforms the entire setting into a billowing, whale-strewn ocean. At the end of the play they row an imaginary whaleboat at Fregatte's command after whale-cows, leaving the locomotive to be set into motion by a simple, rustic cowherd, Axel. Neither Pempelfort nor Krudewil, nor for that matter Fregatte, demonstrates the power of equilibrium demanded of a poet. It is Axel who has undergone a sea-change, who transforms the scene.

It may seem puzzling that this nonsense can be called a paraphrase of an essay whose subject is content and form. But the nonsense is embodied in the two erstwhile poets and their bossy playmate; each represents the mere amusement of purely whimsical and intellectual fantasy. The unriddling of the puzzle is presented in the figure of the painter Kotschenreuther, who acts as the mentor of Axel. At the very beginning of the play Axel comes upon the painter intent on the meadow before his easel on which a seascape with a frigate is taking shape. Axel wonders nonplussed why the painter is not setting down the bucolic scene before him, and Kotschenreuther reprimands and instructs him:

4. Tank, p. 50.

Kotschenreuther (*stands up, compares his picture with the landscape*):

You've got to attune yourself to the new spirit. You've got to dive down under the old values . . . Then you'll discover new aspects, sensitive instruments, prophetic mechanisms, a virgin continent . . . and first of all you've got to throw all these stupid titles overboard. Cow, ship, painter, buttercup. They're all delusions, hallucinations, complexes. Do you think your cow minds if you call it a sailboat . . . or even a steamer?

Axel:

You may be right. But what about my eyes? When I look and see—here a cow and there a ship . . .

Kotschenreuther:

That's just it, that's the big mistake. You look at things with your intellect. Keep your simplicity, start all over again from scratch. In the beginning was the ship. Later it developed into a cow, and the cow into a chess set, then the pyramids were built, then came journalism and with it the railroad—who knows what will happen tomorrow.—Bring me some sail juice, I'm thirsty.

Axel:

You mean milk, sir?

Kotschenreuther:

Call it whatever you like, as long as it's as white as Moby Dick.[5]

Axel shows immediate aptness; and his reappearance at the end of the play, with his trusty dog Jonah (which has nothing whatever to do with whales), proves that his gaze has undergone the submersion and the emergence into a world of new potentialities for him. His imagination literally fires the locomotive: It becomes an object (content) which is given its true and proper form. Critics who have read this piece as a call to sanity and reality have sorely missed the point and are off chasing their own fantastic white whales. It is a call to poetry, to the abandonment of what is traditionally held to be the union of content and form (flower equals metaphor for death, shrouded in a "poetic" line; any well-read layman can supply dozens of other possibilities). The play is a call to discovery, to realization, to the application of the perhaps rude but adept hand that will invest content with harmonious form, however outlandish it may seem at a glance.

5. Grass, *Four Plays*, p. 168.

Not only objects present a resistance to form: Non-objective, abstract content, too, can be "drawn into the dialectical game, becomes an object itself; it voids the void into which what is abstract threatens to dissolve: the poem *Diana* . . . composes this process . . . in an image."[6] The poem "Diana —or the Objects" is from the collection *Gleisdreieck*. With a sure hand, with the transposed hand of a graphic artist, Grass limns the huntress Diana on the chase among her hounds, bow drawn, arrow quivering; and her target is the soul of the artist, normally a non-objective concept but to Diana (objectified and photographable) object enough for an unerring bow.

> I have always refused
> to let my shadow-casting body
> to be hurt by a shadowless idea.

> But you, Diana,
> with your bow,
> are to me objective and answerable.[7]

> . . . .

> Immer lehnte ich ab,
> von einer schattenlosen Idee
> meinen schattenwerfenden Körper verletzen zu lassen.

> Doch du, Diana,
> mit deinem Bogen
> bist mir gegenständlich und haftbar.

In a peculiar sense Grass makes Diana and her like answerable to him in all his work; but then he becomes himself exposed in his very marrow. He can form the idea of Diana and in forming her becomes in his very essence contextual form, responding to her resistance with his own, creating the tension of balance, combining the objective and the non-objective in a state of artistic equilibrium.

6. Tank, p. 46.
7. Günter Grass, *Selected Poems,* trans. Michael Hamburger and Christopher Middleton (New York: A Helen and Kurt Wolff Book, Harcourt, Brace & World, 1966), in the translation by Christopher Middleton, p. 51. The German text is in Günter Grass, *Gleisdreieck* (Neuwied: Luchterhand, 1960), p. 74.

Grass is unceasingly at play with seen and unseen objects, amusing himself, teasing his reader, expanding possibilities, molding metaphorical objects into fitting new shapes. From the collection *Vorzüge der Windhühner* the poem "Hochwasser"—a parable of man's enigmatic thrill at confrontations with disaster—finds new form in the two-act play of the same name. The play has a deeper dimension, supplied in particular by the addition of two enchanting, all-too-human rats—but the basic standpoint is retained. On the other hand, from *Gleisdreieck*, the naval engagement in the lyric snapshot "The Sea Battle" retains its miniature quality in a prose paraphrase which Grass inserts, almost as an exegetical commentary, in *The Tin Drum*:

> An American aircraft carrier
> and a Gothic cathedral
> simultaneously sank each other
> in the middle of the Pacific.
> To the last
> the young curate played on the organ.
> Now aeroplanes and angels hang in the air
> and have nowhere to land.[8]

>   .   .   .   .

> Ein amerikanischer Flugzeugträger
> und eine gotische Kathedrale
> versenkten sich
> mitten im Stillen Ozean
> gegenseitig.
> Bis zum Schluß
> spielte der junge Vikar auf der Orgel.—
> Nun hängen Flugzeuge und Engel in der Luft
> und können nicht landen.

The ironic metaphor of peace and pacifism of the organ-playing vicar (the embattled anti-aircraft gunner) is extended to the pilot waifs—abandoned angels—and is retained in the prose paraphrase:

8. Grass, *Selected Poems*, in a translation by Michael Hamburger, p. 47; *Gleisdreieck*, p. 39.

In the middle of the Pacific two enormous aircraft carriers, done up to look like Gothic cathedrals, stood face to face, sent up their planes, and simultaneously sank one another. The planes had no place to land, they hovered helplessly and quite allegorically like angels in mid-air, using up their fuel with a terrible din.[9]

Even so domestic and unappealing an object as an overflowing ashtray has found its way into the form of a poem:

Three Weeks Later

When I returned from a trip
and opened up my apartment,
there stood on the table that ashtray
which I had neglected to empty.—
Such a thing cannot be made up for.[10]

. . . .

Drei Wochen Später

Als ich von einer Reise zurückkehrte
und meine Wohnung aufschloß,
stand auf dem Tisch jener Aschenbecher,
den ich auszuleeren versäumt hatte.—
So etwas läßt sich nicht nachholen.

The ashtray, in the collection *Gleisdreieck,* also found its way into graphic form in the latest book of poetry by Grass, *Ausgefragt*—the epitome of content ashamed of its contents, caught again in a poem entitled "Chain Smoking."[11]

From the same collection the poem "Do Something" strikes contextual chords which resound in the latest play by Grass, *Davor* (Uptight), as well

9. Günter Grass, *The Tin Drum,* trans. Ralph Manheim (New York: Pantheon, 1962), p. 385; *Die Blechtrommel* (Neuwied, Luchterhand, 1959), p. 477.
10. My translation into English; *Gleisdreieck,* p. 84.
11. Günter Grass, *Ausgefragt* (Neuwied: Luchterhand, 1967), pp. 48–49.

as in the subsequent projection and elaboration of the play in the novel *örtlich betäubt* (Local Anaesthetic):

> We can't just look on.
> Even if we can't stop anything,
> we must say what we think.
> (Do something. Do something.
> Anything. Do something then.)
> Indignation, annoyance, rage looked for adjectives.
> Indignation called itself righteous.
> Soon people spoke of everyday annoyance.
> Rage fell into impotence: impotent rage.
> I speak of the protest poem
> and against the protest poem.
> (Once I saw recruits taking the oath
> unswear it behind their backs with crossed fingers.)
> Impotently I protest against impotent protests.
> What I mean is Easter, silence and peace marches.
> What I mean is the hundred good names
> underneath seven true sentences.
> What I mean is guitars and similar
> protest instruments conducive to records.
> I speak of the wooden sword and the missing tooth,
> of the protest poem.
>
> Just as steel has its booms, so poetry has its booms.
> Rearmament opens markets for anti-war poems.
> The cost of production is low.
> Take an eighth of righteous indignation,
> two eighths of everyday annoyance
> and five eighths—to heighten the flavour—of impotent rage.
> For medium-sized feelings against the war
> are cheaply obtained
> and have been shopspoiled ever since Troy.
> (Do something. Do something.
> Anything. Do something then.)[12]

12. Günter Grass, *New Poems*, trans. Michael Hamburger (New York: A Helen and Kurt Wolff Book, Harcourt, Brace & World, 1968), p. 39, with facing German text on p. 38; original German text, *Ausgefragt*, p. 59.

Irgendwas machen

Da können wir doch nicht zusehen.
Wenn wir auch nichts verhindern,
wir müssen uns deutlich machen.
(Mach doch was. Mach doch was.
Irgendwas. Mach doch was.)
Zorn, Ärger und Wut suchten sich ihre Adjektive.
Der Zorn nannte sich gerecht.
Bald sprach man vom alltäglichen Ärger.
Die Wut fiel in Ohnmacht: ohnmächtige Wut.
Ich spreche vom Protestgedicht
und gegen das Protestgedicht.
(Einmal sah ich Rekruten beim Eid
mit Kreuzfingern hinterrücks abschwören.)
Ohnmächtig protestiere ich gegen ohnmächtige Proteste.
Es handelt sich um Oster-, Schweige- und Friedensmärsche.
Es handelt sich um die hundert guten Namen
unter sieben richtigen Sätzen.
Es handelt sich um Guitarren und ähnliche
die Schallplatte fördernde Protestinstrumente.
Ich rede vom hölzernen Schwert und vom fehlenden Zahn,
vom Protestgedicht.

Wie Stahl seine Konjunktur hat, hat Lyrik ihre Konjunktur.
Aufrüstung öffnet Märkte für Antikriegsgedichte.
Die Herstellungskosten sind gering.
Man nehme: ein Achtel gerechten Zorn,
zwei Achtel alltäglichen Ärger
und fünf Achtel, damit sie vorschmeckt, ohnmächtige Wut.
Denn mittelgroße Gefühle gegen den Krieg
sind billig zu haben
und seit Troja schon Ladenhüter.
(Mach doch was. Mach doch was.
Irgendwas. Mach doch was.)

In the novel, the play, and the poem (which continues for three and a half pages beyond the excerpt given) the same phrases and attitudes are apparent: the compulsion to protest and the lack of the proper vehicle for protest, the search for the proper recipe, the exhortation (which remains un-

answered) to do something so that something will happen. In all instances
the balance is maintained: Talk prevents action, conversation resists confrontation, rage is held in impotent check. Nothing is solved in the end, and
that is just the point: There is no final answer, only the ever present fencing
of question and answer, the effort to fill the pauses. Even the void is full of
content for Grass.

Landscape is one object avoided by Grass, given at most a cursory glance
from a traveling vehicle—car, train, plane—with the exception of a remarkable poem from *Ausgefragt*:

Vermont

For instance green. A green at odds with green.
Green creeps uphill and wins itself a market;
here houses painted white go for a song.

Whoever thought this up discovers
new green for instance in perpetual
instalments, never repeats himself.

Tools lie around, all greenly overcome
though rust had been their reddest resolution,
iron when formed, now to be bought as scrap.

We burned our way through woods, but the new green
grew far too fast, much faster than
and greener than for instance red.

When this same green is broken up.
For instance autumn: the woods put on
their head adornments and migrate.

Once I was in Vermont, there it is green . . .[13]

·   ·   ·   ·   ·   ·   ·

Zum Beispiel Grün. In sich zerstritten Grün.
Grün kriecht bergan, erobert seinen Markt;
so billig sind geweißte Häuser hier zu haben.

Wer sich dies ausgedacht, dem fällt
zum Beispiel immer neues Grün
in Raten ein, der wiederholt sich nie.

13. Grass, *New Poems*, p. 79; *Ausgefragt*, p. 97.

Geräte ruhen, grünlich überwunden,
dabei war Rost ihr rötester Beschluß,
der eisern vorlag, nun als Schrott zu haben.

Wir schlugen Feuerschneisen, doch es wuchs
das neue Grün viel schneller als
und grüner als zum Beispiel Rot.

Wenn dieses Grün erbrochen wird.
Zum Beispiel Herbst: die Wälder legen
den Kopfschmuck an und wandern aus.

Ich war mal in Vermont, dort ist es grün...

Even in this poem, green—hardly an object—contests with more preferred
Grass colors, white and red. Both become objectified, assume form in objects until fall finally vanquishes green, the woods wander off wearing gay
bonnets, and the reader has met the seasons in Vermont, a non-objective
concept which has its correlative objectifization in natural form.

The secret of the skillful balancing act accomplished by Grass is contained in more than one poem or piece of prose. Actually it is visible just
beneath the surface in all that he has written and drawn. Many readers and
critics alike have taken the visibility for their own reflection and thus have
fallen victim to the enormous joke Grass plays repeatedly and intentionally.
On occasion he has, however, been overt—as overt as he can be and maintain his own artistic integrity—about the recipe of his art, the admixture of
form and content in proper proportions. One instance is in the poem "The
Wicked Shoes":

Beauty stands—
and above the applause
the smile trickles, milk
in lidless bowls,
exposed to thundershowers and lemons,
crushed with melancholia, five used-up fingers,
but without intent, prospect of success.

An outing of young girls in April,
with throats which suffer from drafts.

These heads now decapitated,
only columns remain, the Acropolis.
The hats have fled, capitals,
a beer left standing,—beauty endures
in pointed shoes, relevé.

So slowly does happiness leap,
plain to Sunday hunters.
With white hands, such crushed flowers,
that one can smell the effort, resin.
And sweat from undiscovered recesses,
and tears, hysteria before the mirror,—
afterwards, in the pleasant dressing room.

No, unbearable without you, tobacco,
is this glance in the scene set.
Because what bows and runs out, a clock,
twirls and eyes quiver above,
but spooned-empty, without amiability,
the ante-brilliance afterwards, and the hope for: In a moment.
Now pose again, the warmed-up gesture.
that freezes to a port de bras at 90 degrees.

Who then can resolve this stance
and break the forbidden legs of Venus,
the relaxed legs of the Arctic!
Who will take the wicked, pointed shoes
off of the calloused, old feet
and say to the perishing arabesque;
O do be barefoot, naked and dead.[14]

. . . .

Die bösen Schuhe

Die Schönheit steht—
und oben im Applaus
gerinnt das Lächeln, Milch
in bloßen Schalen,
Gewittern ausgesetzt und der Zitrone,

---

14. My translation into English; Günter Grass, *Die Vorzüge der Windhühner* (Neuwied: Luchterhand, 1956), pp. 58–59.

zerdrückt mit Schwermut, fünf verbrauchten Fingern,
doch ohne Absicht, Aussicht auf Erfolg.

Ein Ausflug junger Mädchen im April,
mit Hälsen, die an Zugluft leiden.
Nun abgeschnitten diese Köpfe,
nur Säulen bleiben, die Akropolis.
Geflüchtet sind die Hüte, Kapitäle,
ein abgestanden Bier,—die Schönheit dauert
in spitzen Schuhen, relevé.

So langsam springt das Glück,
den Sonntagsjägern deutlich.
Mit weißen Händen, so zerbrochnen Blumen,
daß man die Mühe, Kolophonium riecht.
Und Schweiß aus unentdeckten Höhlen,
und Tränen, Hysterie vorm Spiegel,—
danach, in der gemütlichen Garderobe.

Nein, unerträglich ohne dich, Tabak,
ist dieser Blick in die gestellte Szene.
Denn was sich beugt und ausläuft, eine Uhr,
sich dreht und oben wimmeln Augen,
doch leergelöffelt, ohne Freundlichkeit,
den Vorglanz Nachher und die Hoffnung auf: Bis gleich.
Nur wieder Stand, die angewärmte Geste,
die erst bei dreißig Grad zum port de bras gefriert.

Wer löst denn diese Haltung ab
und bricht der Venus unerlaubte,
der Arktis nachgelaßne Beine?
Wer nimmt den krustig alten Füßen
die bösen, spitzen Schuhe ab
und sagt zur Arabesk vorm Sterben:
O sei doch barfuß, nackt und tot.

All the effort and sacrifice of art is contained in these lines: the effort of the artist to achieve the balance required to make beauty endure even for a short time, the sacrifice of self-discipline the artist must undergo to achieve the equilibrium between content and form which conjures the imagination and works the magic.

Grass makes his most overt plea for the balance of content and form, couched still in metaphorical terms, in the essay *The Ballerina*.[15] His point of departure is a print, in the manner of the Commedia dell'arte, which he once caught a glimpse of. It is precisely a poet, in his shabby garret room, who is visited by a miraculous Muse, a ballerina who is caught motionless tip-toed on his table. Grass sets the scene in motion, conjectures about the window entrance and exit of the tiny dancer, considers the possibilities: The ballerina will dance in the room, filling it with pirouettes, informing it with harmony. Or she will leap in a long arc out of the window into the night sky, leaving the table empty. The poet will reach for her (but his hands are incapable of grasping, with paper in the one and a pen in the other); and then he will return to his table; and then he will write; for even these days no poem comes into existence without the help of a Muse (4–5).

The object of the poet's enterprise is the *dance* of the ballerina, not the ballerina herself. Depiction of the ballerina would require his presence in her dressing room where she is no longer the creature of abandonment but is anchored to earth by doubts and regrets and domestic cares. On stage the ballerina is left to her own devices. She is not like the tenor who props himself against a chair in order to support his voice. Support is not the same thing as balance; and on stage the ballerina pits her muscles against the forces of gravity to achieve the equilibrium that releases her momentarily but astonishingly from the banality of earth, an equilibrium that propels her into the realm of art. The ballerina's pirouette is an abstraction which demonstrates art because it is no longer nature—the paper rose has the advantage over all vegetation in that it will never wither. The pirouette is art because the violence of effort, the denial of simple-minded, restricted limbs, the miniscule polishing of empty form suffices for weightless beauty without name (6), the essence of beauty, the abstraction: beauty.

Beauty, then, is an essential property of art—and it is something achieved by discipline. The ballerina in her dressing room, weeping over her bruised and bloody feet, is not art, nor is the earth-bound, barefoot modern dancer in her portrayal of a weeping embryo. As Grass puts it: The ballerina's shoes torture her, but her smile remains effortless (8). The self-discipline of the ballerina is compared to the self-abnegation and asceticism of a nun who has dedicated herself to a particular way of life. The dedication of the ballerina is to art; and her severest critic is the mirror before which she practices, a mirror which expands into the mirror of the audience. Grass makes the point that traditional art has always been the "result of consistent re-

15. Günter Grass, *Die Ballerina* (Berlin: Friedenauer Presse, 1965). Page references are given parenthetically in the text.

striction and never of genial immoderation" (9). Art is tough and survives fashions and popular modes because of its innate insistence on the propriety of the correct relationship of content to form.

The highest art is that which is most unnatural and that which is most perfect in formal aspects. Form itself is the base, then, which has through the ages allowed itself to be experimented with for the sake of art. The insistence of form, at the behest of the whole being of the artist, meets the resistance of content and crystallizes into the harmony of art, a harmony in which the haphazard and the random are rejected. The point of equilibrium is the imaginary spot in space indicated by the little finger of the ballerina (11). Like the soul of the poet as the target of Diana's arrow, the point in space as the target of the ballerina's finger is the fulcrum of perspective from which emanates the embracing balance. It contains beauty, the whole being of art, the stability of objective content and structural form.

GÜNTER GRASS AND THE DILEMMA OF DOCUMENTARY DRAMA

ANDRZEJ WIRTH

1. *Documentary Drama and Its Mixed Forms*

IS GÜNTER GRASS'S "GERMAN TRAGEDY," *Die Plebejer proben den Aufstand* (The Plebeians Rehearse the Uprising), a documentary play? Peter Weiss, an artist radically committed to this allegedly new genre, has defined it in an arbitrary way:

> Documentary theater is only theater which constructs the plot solely on the basis of authentic documents. All other theaters are secondary manifestations, which have nothing more to do with documentary theater directly.[1]

This definition applied to Grass's play would exclude it from the documentary genre, since Grass develops his plot on the basis of a fictive situation: the rehearsal of Shakespeare's *Coriolanus,* during the Berlin Uprising in 1953, by a prominent German director who possesses many features of Bertolt Brecht. With our knowledge of the documentary drama, as developed in the sixties, we are more inclined to expand its definition than to exclude Grass's play from this trend. We sense in his play a mixed form, a documentary and fictional drama, not too unlike Rolf Hochhuth's *Der Stellvertreter* (The Deputy), which gave this trend its name.

In both plays the use of documentary material is artistic, i.e., it is transformed, and unified in the structure of a totally new work. In Grass's play we are dealing with specific kinds of "documents," mostly with artistic texts (Shakespeare's *Coriolanus,* Brecht's *Coriolan,* Brecht's poems) which have been transformed into Grass texts through their stylistic reinterpretation.

The term "documentary theater" applies easily to authors like Heinar Kipphardt or Weiss. In Kipphardt's Oppenheimer play, as well as in Weiss's

---

1. *Brecht-Dialog, 1968: Politik auf dem Theater,* ed. Werner Hecht (Munich: Rogner & Bernhard, 1969), p. 108:
    Das dokumentarische Theater ist einzig und allein das Theater, das die Handlung ausschließlich auf authentischen Dokumenten aufbaut, und alle anderen Theater sind schon wieder Erscheinungsformen, die nichts mehr direkt mit dem dokumentarischen Theater zu tun haben.

Die Ermittlung (The Investigation) and his Vietnam play, the documentary material directly determines the structure of the drama. In Hochhuth's or in Grass's play the documentary material does not directly affect the structure and the content. It does not prevent Hochhuth from following the formal patterns of a traditional Schiller dramaturgy; it does not prevent Grass (who in langauge is indebted also to Schiller) from mixing the traditional approach of the "drama of ideas" (Ideendrama) with a modern absurdist sensitivity. In both cases the document is used as a source of inspiration and disappears behind the reality of the play.

In a discussion with Herbert Lindenberger of Stanford another typology, based on the treatment of the protagonist, was proposed. According to it, the documentary drama exposes its protagonist as a villain (Mulka, Boger), or as a martyr (Oppenheimer, Hammarskjold), or as a respected figure in the moment of a failure which jeopardizes this respect (Pius XII, Churchill). Grass, with his Boss taken justly or unjustly for B.B., seems to belong to the latter category.

2. *The Historical Event as Seen by Brecht and Grass*

The subtitle of the play, "A German Tragedy," seems to indicate, however, that the play deals more with the historical event—the Berlin Uprising of 1953—than with the protagonist, constructed from biographical and bibliographical allusions to Bertolt Brecht. Taking this assumption as a working hypothesis, let us examine Brecht's and Grass's perception of this historical event.

In a statement which Brecht addressed to the events of June, 1953, we read:

> The demonstrations of June 17th showed the dissatisfaction of a considerable percentage of the Berlin working class with a series of unsuccessful economic measures. Organized fascist elements tried to misuse this dissatisfaction for their own sanguinary purposes. For several hours Berlin stood on the brink of a third world war. Thanks only to the quick and competent intervention of Soviet troops were these attempts thwarted.[2]

2. Bertolt Brecht, *Werkausgabe,* in *Gesammelte Werke* (Munich: Suhrkamp, 1967), XX, 327:
Die Demonstranten des 17. Juni zeigten die Unzufriedenheit eines beträchtlichen Teils der Berliner Arbeiterschaft mit einer Reihe verfehlter wirtschaftlicher Maßnahmen. Organisierte faschistische Elemente versuchten, diese Unzufriedenheit für ihre blutigen Zwecke zu mißbrauchen. Mehrere Stunden stand Berlin am Rande eines dritten Weltkrieges. Nur dem schnellen und sicheren Eingreifen sowjetischer Truppen ist es zu verdanken, daß diese Versuche vereitelt wurden.

Although some formulations in this text are almost identical with the official version of the SED, there is no reason to believe that they are not an expression of Brecht's genuine convictions. His loyalty to the East German Republic, which he considered to be the first German workers state, was unshaken. Many years had passed since the period of the *Lehrstücke*, his didactic plays, when he still considered the possibility of a permanent revolution. After his play *Tage der Kommune* (Days of the Commune, 1949) there was no doubt that he, not only in his political beliefs but also in his artistic works, was voicing another solution: after the revolution—a suppressive state, made up of workers, a dictatorship of the proletariat. (Brecht's work on this drama and his decision to live in East Germany may coincide.) The danger of a third world war as a possible implication of the Berlin demonstrations does not seem to be a mere political phrase when used by Brecht, since he interpreted the demand for free elections in Germany as leading subsequently to a great war:

> The kind of elections we had in Germany cannot have been very good. Twice in my own lifetime the Germans, in the civilized manner of which we speak, voted for war. Twice, through "free elections," they endorsed governments which not only plotted criminal wars but also lost them.[3]

In Brecht's perception, June 17th was not a revolution; it was an aberation caused by workers who were unable to understand their own interests. Transforming this formula, using the alienated (verfremdet) form of the historical tense, Brecht wrote:

> The workers, at first still partly alarmed about the new tempo of work which was necessary for a decisive increase in production, have since become aware that this production is for the benefit of all, and the competition of ideas and forces is in full swing, and growing.[4]

One of the main motifs of Brecht's work in the thirties was his debate with social reformism. His attitude toward it, as *Die heilige Johanna der*

3. Ibid., XX, 328:
Die Art der Wahlen, wie wir sie in Deutschland hatten, kann nicht ganz gut gewesen sein. Zweimal während meines Lebens wählten die Deutschen in jener zivilisierten Weise, von der die Rede ist, den Krieg. Zweimal bestätigten sie durch "freie Wahlen" Regierungen, die verbrecherische Kriege anzettelten und sie außerdem noch verloren.
4. Ibid., XX, 319:
Die Arbeiter, am Anfang zum Teil noch erschreckt über das neue Arbeitstempo, das zu einer entscheidenden Steigerung der Produktion nötig war, haben einzusehen gelernt, daß diese Produktion ihnen allen zugute kommt, und der Wettbewerb der Ideen und Kräfte ist [in] vollem und zunehmendem Schwung.

Schlachthöfe (Saint Joan of the Stockyards, 1931) indicates, was a radical refusal. There is no way to reform capitalism; it has to be destroyed. That could occur only by means of the socialist revolution. Brecht did not anticipate an evolutionary path to socialism ("Small changes are the foes of great changes"). Once socialism was established, it did not need any more internal revolutions; it was to perfect itself *ex definitione*. A revolution to improve socialism would be, for the late Brecht, a contradiction in terms. In the twenties he sympathized with the concept of the permanent revolution in the *Badener Lehrstück vom Einverständnis* (The Baden-Baden Didactic Play of Acquiescence, 1929), but soon shifted to the Leninist orthodox interpretation of the socialist revolution as resulting in the dictatorship of the proletariat. Even if not satisfactory in its present practice, socialism, Brecht believed, does have self-correcting impetus, while there is no way to correct capitalism. The Maoist concept of the "counterrevolution from the left" against the petrifying tendencies of the party apparatus belongs to the post-Brechtian era and found its theorists outside of China in Eastern Europe (Kolakowski, Kuron, Modzelewski, and the pro-Dubček movement in Czechoslovakia).

In his campaign speech for the German Socialist Party (SPD), "Was ist des Deutschen Vaterland?" (What is the German Fatherland?, 1965), Grass defines the events of 1953 as follows:

> On the 16th and 17th of June, 1953, an uprising of German workers took place in East Berlin, and in the Soviet-occupied zone. In its strongest moments—at the beginning on the Stalinallee, and at its moment of defeat—it bore clear social-democratic features and caused Walter Ulbricht's dictatorship to totter, if only for a few hours. This uprising of the workers was falsified into an attempted fascist riot by the DDR, and into a popular insurrection by West German officialdom, even though it can be easily proved that—with a few praiseworthy exceptions—the farmers, office workers, and intellectuals remained at home.[5]

5. Günter Grass, *Über das Selbstverständliche* (Neuwied: Luchterhand, 1968), p. 44:
Am 16. und 17. Juni 1953 fand in Ostberlin und in der sowjetisch besetzten Zone ein deutscher Arbeiteraufstand statt, der in seinen stärksten Momenten, im Beginn an der Stalinallee wie im Scheitern, deutlich sozialdemokratische Züge trug und Walter Ulbrichts Diktatur, wenn auch nur für Stunden, ins Wanken brachte. Dieser Arbeiteraufstand ist von der DDR-Regierung zum faschistischen Putschversuch und von verantwortlicher deutscher Seite zu einer Volkserhebung verfälscht worden, obgleich sich ohne Mühe beweisen läßt, daß das Bürgertum und die Bauern, Beamte und Intellektuelle bis auf löbliche Ausnahmen zu Hause geblieben sind. (My translation)

It is obvious that we are confronted with two extremely different, irreconcilable political points of view. For Brecht, Grass would represent the bourgeois reformist. For Grass, Brecht is a Hegelian dogmatist. Only in Grass's play does the Boss (Brecht) discover in himself, for a moment, the sensitivity of the contemporary neo-Marxist revisionist. (Thus the figure of the Boss, in his "moment of weakness," is an anticipation of the 'sixties.)

For Grass, Hegel is suspect because of his *Machtstaatslehre* (theory of the power state), and Stalin as well as Hitler appear to him to have been students of Hegel. Refusing Hegel, Grass defines himself as a reformist, as a social democrat; reformism, as we know, was Brecht's archenemy. Grass is not afraid to discuss the fate of Germany in the categories of German *Volk* and German Nation. For Brecht the notion "folk" and "nation" were suspect: "Let's stop talking about nation and people and talk about the populace."[6]

There are not only objective differences between political positions and political temperaments; the generation gap cannot be overlooked as a determining factor. Seen from this perspective, Brecht with his Hegelian Marxism appears as a typical product of the post-World War I period, while Grass projects on the Boss features of the neo-Marxist of the 'sixties. It seems that certain leftist dogmatic attitudes of the twenties and the thirties are inconceivable for the Grass generation, which judges socialism comparatively on the basis of its post-World War II reality:

> . . . a corrupted Communism that has developed into a dictatorship of the bureaucracy is confronted by democracies whose parliaments are subservient to lobbies, whose formally free elections have more and more become a farce.[7]

Referring to dictatorship, Brecht wrote: "Those dictatorships which take measures against conditions of an economic nature must be supported and endured."[8] For this reason the equation between Stalin and Hitler would be impossible for Brecht.

6. Brecht, *Werkausgabe*, XX, 313:
Reden wir eine Zeitlang nicht mehr vom Volk. Reden wir von der Bevölkerung.
7. Günter Grass, *Speak Out!*, trans. Ralph Manheim (New York: A Helen and Kurt Wolff Book, Harcourt, Brace & World [1968]). p. 109; Über das Selbstverständliche, p. 221:
. . . einem korrumpierten Kommunismus, der sich zur Diktatur der Bürokratie entwickelt hat, stehen Demokratien gegenüber, deren Parlamente interessenhörig geworden sind, deren formalfreiheitliche Wahlen mehr und mehr zur Farce werden.
8. Brecht, *Werkausgabe*, XX, 102:
Es müssen jene Diktaturen unterstützt und ertragen werden, welche gegen die Zustände ökonomischer Art vorgehen.

Let us summarize. Analyzing Grass's play as a semi-documentary drama based on a real historical event, it is necessary to be aware that: The Berlin Uprising had a totally different meaning for Brecht than for Grass, and the Boss's perception of the Uprising does not represent Brecht's perception of this event.

3. *The Test of the Reception*

In Berlin's Schiller Theater Grass's *Plebeians* tested Bertolt Brecht's credibility *vis à vis* the Uprising. The outcome of this test was a negative one. The Boss was a *Versager* (failure), a Hamletic victim of his own theorems which confused his insights of reality. The Berlin Uprising was a kind of delayed French Revolution, crying in vain for a spiritual leader. For the Berlin audience there was no doubt that the Boss was Bertolt Brecht, that his theater is "am Schiffbauerdamm," that Erwin is Erich Engel, Kozanka is Kuba Barthel, Volumnia is Helene Weigel, etc. The director, Hansjörg Utzerath, advised by the author, did not succeed in abolishing the impression that the case of B.B. and June 17th is under discussion. And the Berlin audience interpreted the play as a challenge to Bertolt Brecht's image, as a case of Günter Grass versus Bertolt Brecht. Especially for the younger generation, for which Brecht had become an idol and which at the same time was sympathetic to Grass, the *Plebeians* marked a shift to a reactionary camp. The leftist press launched its accusations of anti-communism immediately.[9] The general impression after the Berlin premiere was that Grass, by challenging Brecht, was attempting to establish himself *vis à vis* Brecht as *the* national German writer, as Brecht had once attempted to establish himself *vis à vis* Gerhart Hauptmann and Georg Kaiser.

Grass was unhappy about such reactions, since he thinks of his play as a free adaptation of history. He forgets, however, that it is one thing to adapt the case of the historical Coriolanus as Brecht did, and another to adapt the case of Brecht as, on the basis of the Berlin production, it seemed he was attempting. For the German audience, Brecht is not a forgotten historical or half-legendary figure like Coriolanus. For them, Grass's play, loaded with Brecht biographica and with allusions to his work, was about the controversial B.B. and aimed at destroying his nimbus.

Is it possible to move away from the theatricalization of Brecht's case

---

9. "In der Sackgasse des Antikommunismus," in *Der Morgen*, Berlin, January 21, 1966.

toward a more universal stage interpretation? In Germany such an attempt would seem to be very difficult.

The American premiere of *The Plebeians Rehearse the Uprising* (1967) in the Harvard Dramatic Club presented an interesting alternative. The director, Timothy Swayze Mayer, dropped the Shakespeare-Coriolanus notion and avoided, as far as the text permitted it, allusions to Brecht himself. It is obvious that the English translation makes this easier than the German original, in which Grass succeeds in recreating a geniune Brechtian idiom. In the Harvard production *Coriolanus* was not staged as an Elizabethan play but as a Chinese opera, heightening the effect of the theater within a theater. Dean Gitter in playing the lead eliminated from his appearance any resemblance to Bertolt Brecht.

Through such changes, the stage was no longer a tribunal for a specific discussion of B.B. versus the 1953 Berlin Uprising. The play succeeded in exposing a more universal theme—the dilemma of the artist: the aesthetic man versus the man of action, art versus reality, theory versus practice, ideal versus reality. The linguistic and cultural distance between two nations facilitated the more universal rendering. The "German Tragedy" became a nationally undefined social drama with sufficient background to allow for the artist's dilemma. The production not only ignored the Brechtian and Shakespearian aspects, it also missed the inherent interplay between Coriolanus and the Boss. The play was thus more impoverished than embellished, in order to arrive at this more universal reading.

Grass assumed that "the case of Brecht and the case of Sir Walter Raleigh seem to encourage the falsification of theatrical history and of English-Roman history for the benefit of historical drama."[10] Grass has written, however, not a historical but a contemporary drama. His figures are still alive, or died recently, which according to Weiss's definition is one characteristic of the documentary drama. Grass's analogy is false. Even if Raleigh was the model for Shakespeare's Coriolanus, Raleigh does not appear on the stage, just as Stalin does not appear in Brecht's adaptation of *Coriolanus*; Grass's protagonist is unmistakably Brecht.

The objective development of European drama in the sixties is not without importance here. The documentary drama, as initiated by Hochhuth's

10. Günter Grass, "The Prehistory and Posthistory of the Tragedy of *Coriolanus* from Livy and Plutarch via Shakespeare down to Brecht and Myself," in *The Plebeians Rehearse the Uprising*, trans. Ralph Manheim (New York: A Helen and Kurt Wolff Book, Harcourt, Brace & World [1966]), p. xxxiv; "Vor- und Nachgeschichte der Tragödie des Coriolanus von Livius und Plutarch über Shakespeare bis zu Brecht und mir," *Akzente*, 11 (1964), 219:
>   Der Fall Brecht und der Fall Sir Walter Raleigh erlauben und erlaubten Fälschungen der Theatergeschichte und der englisch-römischen Geschichte zu Gunsten der jeweiligen Historienstücke.

The Deputy (1962) and continued by Kipphardt with his *In the Matter of J. Robert Oppenheimer* (1964), and Weiss with his *The Investigation* (1965), annexed for this new genre contemporary figures whose roles seemed to endow them with "historical" relevance (Pius XII, the physicist Oppenheimer, Boger and Mulka as a new type of criminal). Grass's play was automatically received as a documentary play about Bertolt Brecht and the Berlin Uprising. Grass's claim, in answer to his critics after the Berlin premiere that his play discusses a universal issue and should be judged as such, sounded unconvincing—almost as if Hochhuth were to insist that *The Deputy* does not present the case of Pius XII but rather the universal problem of the Church's moral responsibility.

Despite all the difficulties mentioned here, it seems that there remains another possible reading and staging of the *Plebeians,* which would stress the universality of its problems.

4. *Grass's Adaptation of* Coriolanus

Grass is very critical of Brecht's adaptation of *Coriolanus,* in contrast to his adaptation of Marlowe's *Life of Edward II of England.* Of Brecht's *Coriolan* Grass writes: "His version has deprived the tragedy of its naïve plot and replaced it with a hard-working mechanism, which does its stint and makes its partisanship sound pleasantly aesthetic."[11] Grass, however, is not judging Brecht's results according to Brecht's prerequisites and goals. The *Coriolanus* adaptation was done specifically for the Berlin Ensemble production, not as a universal proposal, and as such worked quite well in the 1964 Wekwerth/Tenschert production. The reduction of the hero's complexity and the dissolution of the tragedy into the form of an epic chronicle were two goals of the adaptation; thus it should be judged according to the standards of Brecht's aesthetics.

The critics have underestimated the importance of Shakespeare's *Coriolanus,* greatly stressed in Grass's address at the Academy of Arts and Letters in 1964 in Berlin, "The Prehistory and Posthistory of the Tragedy of Coriolanus from Livy and Plutarch via Shakespeare to Brecht and Myself." It allowed the author to make the most of the "theater within a theater"

11. Grass, "Prehistory," p. xxii; "Vor- und Nachgeschichte," p. 208:
Seine Fassung hat der Tragödie das naive Gefälle genommen und an dessen Stelle einen fleißigen Mechanismus gesetzt, der zwar sein Soll erfüllt und die gewollte Tendenz geschmackvoll ästhetisiert.

technique with all its philosophical (art versus reality) and linguistic (Shakespearian versus contemporary idiom) implications. Brecht's occupation with Shakespeare also gave Grass's play its central metaphor. Grass substitutes Shakespeare for reality, and the whole experience of the protagonist is expressed through this metaphor. The question-answer (Act I, Scene 1)— "Why do we change Shakespeare? . . . Because . . . we can."[12]—results (Act IV, Scene 4) in the recognition: "that we . . . can't change Shakespeare unless we change ourselves."[13] This is probably the most universal statement carried by the play. Applied to the protagonist it means that his Marxist belief that we change ourselves by changing the world (as expressed in Brecht's didactic plays) was transformed into the conviction (which Brecht considered idealistic) that we have to change ourselves in order to change the world. Between these two poles of activism and moralism Grass sets the rehearsal of the Uprising.

Grass builds his plays around a central image. In *Hochwasser* (Flood) it is the "end of the rainy season and the beginning of the Ice Age," in *Noch zehn Minuten bis Buffalo* (Only Ten Minutes to Buffalo) the locomotive, in *Die bösen Köche* (The Wicked Cooks) the recipe, in *Davor* (Uptight) dentistry.

The parable, a favorite form of Brecht's, is treated critically, and not without irony, by Grass. The belly parable, denounced as solidaristic, finally saves the Boss's and Erwin's lives. Grass, the image-maker, speaks here against Brecht, the parable-maker:

> I'd tickle you both pro and con,
> with the same blade of straw for argument . . .[14]

The central image of the *Plebeians* is Coriolanus. Coriolanus is the Boss, Coriolanus is Stalin, and Coriolanus is life itself. This image-within-an-image device is typical of the Theater of the Absurd. Coriolanus's arbitrariness reflects an attitude similar to that of an intellectual ("his own worst enemy"); his unwillingness to resign—the attitude of a dictator; his resistance to change—life itself ("colossal, bigger-than-life").

---

12. Grass, *Plebeians*, p. 5; *Plebejer*, p. 8:
Warum ändern wir Shakespeare? . . . Weil wir ihn ändern können.
13. Grass, *Plebeians*, p. 103; *Plebejer*, p. 100:
. . . daß wir . . . den Shakespeare nicht ändern können, solange wir uns nicht ändern.
14. Grass, *Plebeians*, p. 10; *Plebejer*, p. 12:
Euch beide könnt' ich für und gegen kitzeln,
mit gleichem Strohhalm-Argument.

Grass vacillates between a classical and an absurdist treatment of his subject. The Boss appears in his play, as in a traditional *Ideendrama* (drama of ideas), as a real partner of history, as somebody upon whose decision the fate of the nation hangs.

This concept of the writer as a national leader was foreign to Brecht. In his *Marxist Studies* (1926–1939), the question—"Why does the proletariat need intellectuals?"—is answered as follows: "1. In order to punch bourgeois ideologies full of holes; 2. In order to study the forces which move the world; 3. In order to further develop abstract theory."[15] There is no place in this concept for political leadership.

Apparently Brecht and Grass have contradictory views of the role of the writer. While Brecht throughout the years trained himself in submission to the will of the political collective, represented by the party, Grass thinks of himself, in a more traditional way, as a national writer of "both Germanys." Thus the elevation of the writer's role to that of a leading figure of national life in the *Plebeians* is rather foreign to Brecht. Giving key importance to the figure of the writer in his play, Grass is reflecting his own notion of the writer's position, not Brecht's.

Elevated to such importance, the Boss is both a tragic and a comic figure. He is tragic because of his self-confinement in theory, which has—as we are asked to believe—such important social consequences. He is comic because of his inability to change. Paradoxically enough, the Boss shares this tragicomical quality with Shakespeare's and even more with Brecht's Coriolanus. In Shakespeare's play and in Brecht's adaptation, Coriolanus's decisions have influence on the survival of Roman society, and this element gives the figure a tragic stature. It is difficult to believe that the action or non-action of the Boss could really influence the fate of the Uprising. In this respect Grass unintentionally represents the reality of the Uprising, which could not be helped because of the lack of an organizational basis.

The "German Tragedy" does not seem to be the tragedy of the Boss. He is consistent and, with the exception of one short sentimental moment with the Hairdresser ("ein Gedicht lang," for the length of a poem), does not see alternatives to his behavior. After all, his skepticism of this "clumsy" revolt is confirmed by reality. He has no partners except the imaginary figure of Coriolanus. Neither the rather infantile workers, in whom the Boss hesitates to see agents of real change, nor the Establishment's speaker Kozanka with his grotesque appearance could be considered partners.

15. Brecht, *Werkausgabe*, XX, 54:
Wozu braucht das Proletariat die Intellektuellen?
1. Um die bürgerliche Ideologie zu durchlöchern; 2. Zum Studium der Kräfte, die die Welt bewegen; 3. Um die reine Theorie weiterzuentwickeln.

Is, then, the "German Tragedy" the tragedy of the Uprising? The Uprising takes place backstage. The confrontation between the socialist establishment and the workers is compromised through their infantilism and even more through the Boss's critical but realistic reception of their undertaking. The confrontation takes the form of a grotesque and funny slogan-duel between the worker Wiebe and Kozanka's voice, heard through a megaphone. This confrontation obviously lacks a tragic quality; and the subtitle "A German Tragedy" should rather be interpreted as an ironical statement on the historically recognized German inability for genuine social revolution.

On the flyleaf of the German edition we read: "17. Juni 1953: Datum einer deutschen, also gescheiterten Revolution" (17 June 1953: The date of a German, thus a miscarried revolution). Does this mean that the author shares the Boss's fatalistic conviction about the German inability to act as revolutionaries? It would seem that on this point he is much less skeptical than the Boss.

Through the confrontation between the Boss and the Uprising Grass's drama tends to become a semi-documentary play similar to the type established by Hochhuth's *The Deputy*. Both expose a highly respected figure in the moment of a failure (in both cases a result of non-action) which jeopardizes this respect. The theme was obviously pushing Grass in this "revisionistic" direction; perhaps also the temptation to establish himself as the national writer *vis à vis* the last influential *praeceptor Germaniae*. Grass avoided, however, the scandalizing effect of the documentary school and its dilemmas; that is to say, the Boss in his play is not a fallen angel, or a villain, even less a martyr.

5. *Coriolanus and the Syndrome of the Contemporary Intellectual*

The play gains its stature through the very effective Coriolanus-image, and especially through the juxtaposition and partial identification of the Boss and Coriolanus. Using the Coriolanus-image in this twofold function, Grass gives his "German Tragedy" a universal touch. The dialectic of excellence is the same for the man of action (Coriolanus) as it is for the man of reflection (the Boss—the artist and thinker): The necessary specialization carries with it the destructive seeds of onesidedness. This dialectic seems to apply to Coriolanus as well as to the Boss. Noticing this, Grass made creative use of it in his "adaptation of Shakespeare."

The Boss, a Hegelian "Besserwisser" (know-it-all), follows his own theorems with such indulgence that reality gradually disappears behind them. This perception seems to fit perfectly the image of the real Brecht as it emerges from the posthumously published works. The frightening definition of Stalinism in *Me-ti, Buch der Wendungen* (Me-ti, Book of Changes) could serve as an example of such trap-theorems:

> Bread is thrown with such vehemence among the people that many are killed. The most prosperous institutions are created by scoundrels, and too many virtuous people block progress.[16]

For this kind of "dialectical mentality," Grass found a genuine idiom, which, being his own, remains unmistakably "Brechtian":

> Erwin:
> > Resolved to kill the enemy of the people—
> > That's right, that's what it says—Coriolanus.
> Boss:
> > Who has well served his country!
> > The people can't check off his scars on all
> > The fingers of both hands.[17]

The heroism of Shakespeare's Coriolanus leads to the betrayal of Rome; the Boss's mastery of dialectics leads to the betrayal of his own cause. Coriolanus's patriotism and his contempt for the people finds an equivalent in the Boss's affection for the working class and his scathing contempt for the workers (beer-table strategists). Even Coriolanus's mother-fixation finds an analogy in the submission of the Boss to Volumnia. Just as Coriolanus sees himself as a good citizen, the Boss sees himself as the only competent revolutionary; Coriolanus's contempt for solicited popularity is similar to the unresponsiveness of the Boss to easy popularity. Coriolanus's behavior appears intolerable, but in the end he has acted for the best, just as the seemingly

---

16. Bertolt Brecht, *Me-ti. Buch der Wendungen. Fragment,* ed. Uwe Johnson (Frankfurt/Main: Suhrkamp, 1965), p. 126:
Das Brot wird mit solcher Wut ins Volk geworfen, daß es viele erschlägt. Die segensreichsten Einrichtungen werden von Schurken geschaffen, und nicht wenige tugendhafte Leute stehen dem Fortschritt im Wege.
17. Grass, *Plebeians,* p. 8; *Plebejer,* p. 10:
Erwin:
Und sind entschlossen, totzuschlagen
den Volksfeind—steht hier!—Coriolan.
Chef:
Der sich verdient gemacht!
Das Volk kann seine Narben
an Fingern sich nicht abklavieren.

intolerable behavior of the Boss appears in the end to be realistic. Whereas Coriolanus is devoted to the self-image of a perfect soldier, the Boss is devoted to the cultivation of a self-image of a Chinese sage. The denial of spontaneity in Brecht's Coriolan and in Grass's hero leads to the predictability of their actions: Coriolan is manipulated by his pride; the Boss is manipulated by his own theory. The exaggerated concern with self-image produces its perversion. The patriot becomes a traitor; the ideologist of the working class betrays (we are asked to believe) the workers; modesty degenerates into proud arrogance and the restriction of feelings into outbursts of sentimentality.

The parallelism shown above seems to indicate that Grass's play about Brecht's adaptation of Shakespeare's *Coriolanus*, which Grass found insufficient, is itself an adaptation of Shakespeare, namely, of the Coriolanus syndrome as it applies to a contemporary intellectual. Grass judged Brecht's adaptation of Coriolanus negatively: "Where the spoils are so meager as in the present case, literary piracy does not pay."[18] Whether it paid or not in Brecht's case remains a question of judgment. It seems that literary piracy would have paid even more in Grass's case, if he had managed to refrain from a German *couleur local*. The Coriolanus-Boss analogy made it possible for Grass to free himself partially from the limitations of documentary drama—its concreteness—and to move toward more universal problems. Grass sees the arrogance of a Hegelian know-it-all (My course was right. Only the compass lied),[19] not his aestheticism, as the most striking feature of the contemporary intellectual syndrome.

The epithet "mieser Ästhet" (wretched aesthete) applied to the Boss by Volumnia seems undeserved. An aesthete could not produce the argument used by the Boss while hesitating to write a manifesto for the workers: "Who'd benefit but poetry?"[20] The Boss is, first of all, an intellectual, a theorist; he has to be convinced in order to act; he constantly undergoes the agonies of the notorious Hegelian antinomy: "If I could only be beside myself, but in the swim."[21]

In the last lines of the third act, Grass's play frees itself from the limitations imposed through the controversial case of Brecht and the Berlin Uprising:

18. Grass, "Prehistory," p. xxii; "Vor- und Nachgeschichte," p. 208;
. . . bei so schmaler Beute [lohnte] der Griff nach dem fremden Stoff nicht.
19. Grass, *Plebeians*, p. 51; *Plebejer*, p. 52:
Mein Kurs war richtig, doch der Kompaß log!
20. Grass, *Plebeians*, p. 32; *Plebejer*, p. 32:
Wem, außer der Poesie, wäre damit geholfen?
21. Grass, *Plebeians*, p. 71; *Plebejer*, p. 70:
. . . außer mir, aber dabei sein.

> Benighted children worshiping a dove:
> "Come, Holy Spirit; come abide with us."
> Come, come, my dove, o come sweet reason.
> Come, Holy Spirit, thou the first atheist.
> Don't mind the stairs, take the emergency
> Door, and assail me with relentless hardware.
>
> ·
>
> The Holy Spirit breathed, and I mistook
> It for a draft, and cried:
> Who's come here to molest me?[22]

Here the play reaches into the very heart of an eternal human dilemma: the temptation to make images and the risk to follow them—the eternal drama of theory and practice, of art and reality.

One may ask whether this perception gives the play a tragic quality. In the context of a play about B.B., the question is superfluous. After all, it was Brecht who called Hegel "the greatest humorist of all times."

In the context of a play about Coriolanus, the Boss is to the same degree tragic as Coriolanus; that is to say, the syndrome of the contemporary intellectual unifies tragic and comic features. Although indebted to Schiller, no less than to Hochhuth, Grass, thanks to his absurdist sensitivity, avoids an anachronistic attempt to re-create a Romantic tragedy. For this reason, perhaps, his equating of Coriolanus and the poet is for us enlightening and valid.

---

22. Grass, *Plebeians*, pp. 94–95; *Plebejer*, pp. 91–92:
Verwirrte Kinder beten eine Taube an:
"Komm, heiliger Geist, kehr bei uns ein!"
Komm, meine Taube, komm, Vernunft.
Komm, heiliger Geist, du erster Atheist,
scheu keine Treppen, nimm den Noteingang,
geh mich mit harten Requisiten an.
· · · · · · · · · · · · · · · · ·
Es atmete der heilge Geist.
Ich hielt's für Zugluft,
rief: wer stört!

THE DOGMATISM OF PAIN:
LOCAL ANAESTHETIC

ERHARD FRIEDRICHSMEYER

THE PUBLICATION IN THE SUMMER OF 1969 OF GRASS'S NEW NOVEL, *Local Anaesthetic,* was a major literary event in West Germany. Since the appearance of *Dog Years* six years earlier, the writer had become a star campaigner for the Social Democrats, a much-heard voice in cultural affairs, in short, a public figure of considerable note. Now, in *Local Anaesthetic,* he had returned to prose fiction, still the principal basis of his fame.

In the history of German letters no other serious writer matches the kind of public exposure and fame Grass has attained. In a special sense this speaks more against than for him. Germany traditionally has expected writers to be aloof from worldly affairs. Schiller characterizes this attitude definitively in one of his poems. He envisions Olympus, not the earth, as the writer's true domain.[1] Grass addresses himself to this tradition in his Princeton speech of 1966.[2] With the eloquence of wishful thinking, he pronounces it dead. But that it is very much alive in the public consciousness is implicitly revealed in his contention that the writer is embarrassed at being called a "Dichter" by his admiring public. Moreover, the exaggerated skepticism of Grass's reaction to the question of the writer's political influence testifies to how sensitive he himself is to this prejudice of long standing. To this day, politics and literature do not mix well in West Germany. And in view of the critics' reaction to Grass's new novel, they do not seem to mix at all. In making the campaign circuit with a vengeance equaled by few professionals, Grass had sunk his hands in the political mud. Judging by some of the cutting responses to *Local Anaesthetic*—allegedly concerned with its quality, but much too emotional to be simply aesthetic verdict—Grass was not able

1. "Die Teilung der Erde," *Schillers Werke,* ed. Ludwig Bellermann (Leipzig: Bibliographisches Institut, n.d.), I, 133.

2. Günter Grass, "Vom mangelnden Selbstvertrauen der schreibenden Hofnarren unter Berücksichtigung nicht vorhandener Höfe," *Akzente,* 13 (1966), 194–199; published in English translation by Ralph Manheim under the title "On Writers as Court Jesters and on Non-existent Courts," in Günter Grass, *Speak Out!* (New York: A Helen and Kurt Wolff Book, Harcourt, Brace & World [1968]), pp. 47–53.

to do so with impunity. One of the reviewers, for example, asserts that *Local Anaesthetic* is unoriginal and a typical product of old age.[3]

This comment not only implies that Grass has lost his touch as an artist, but it also has other overtones. Already *The Plebeians Rehearse the Uprising* and more recently *Uptight* had given the critics strong reason to suspect that Grass's political direction would find its way into his future prose works. Their suspicions were compounded by Grass's indication that his new novel would be a twin to his latest play. *Local Anaesthetic,* then, in being a transposition of *Uptight,* proved to be a pre-programmed disappointment. It is indeed a far cry from the vitalistic prose and irrepressible sweep of his earlier novels, which had contributed more than the achievements of any other writer to the rebirth of literature in West Germany. His prose had gained immediate public and critical success in the Western world. To the critic it represented an unanswerable reply to the Marxist assertion that post-war Western literature is only a dying branch on the dying tree of bourgeois art. Moreover, Grass's disdain for ideological involvement in the earlier novels, his special brand of art for art's sake agreed with the prevalent dogmas of Western literary criticism. According to the Russian literary theoretician Myasnikov—who to be sure takes the part for the whole—these tenets include as first and foremost the belief in the autonomy and uniqueness of the work of art as well as the implicit assumption that the work of art is answerable only to itself.[4] Hence Myasnikov sees Western critical categories as favoring purely formal and aesthetic judgments. Grass himself encouraged this mode of criticism for his novels when he denied the presence of meaning in his work and the legitimacy of interpreting his images as cultural and political symbols. "Content," he pronounced, "is the inevitable obstacle, the pretext for form."[5] Grass's earlier novels and his directives for dealing with them exegetically were in accord with the modes of criticism predominant in the West. The publication of *Local Anaesthetic* put an end to this state of affairs.

Its debut was greeted with scores of reviews. *Die Zeit* carried no fewer than three in successive issues. By and large, the important critics were agreed in damning the work. The last of the reviews in *Die Zeit* summarizes the commentary to that date and points to the following four major objections: "Grass is no longer the 'Grass of old.'—Grass should not have pub-

3. Marcel Reich-Ranicki, "Eine Müdeheldensoße," *Die Zeit,* September 2, 1969.

4. Alexander Mjasnikow, "Sozialistischer Realismus und Literaturtheorie," *Sinn und Form,* 19 (1967), 669–716.

5. Günter Grass, "Der Inhalt als Widerstand," *Akzente,* 4 (1957), 229–235 (translation mine).

lished the novel at the time of the election campaign.—Grass's novel is un-interesting because its figures are uninteresting.—Grass's novel to be sure is less interesting than his previous ones, but the reason for this is that our times are damned uninteresting."[6] Points two through four are open to question. Point one is not. All in all, the Grass of *Local Anaesthetic* is not the Grass of old. The orgiastic diction and exorbitant individuality of his style are largely gone. Whereas in *The Tin Drum, Dog Years,* and *Cat and Mouse* the world is violently and sensually refracted, in *Local Anaesthetic* it is in-tellectually, and often painfully, reflected. All this seems to confirm the re-viewers' position. If one applies the standards of his earlier prose, *Local Anaesthetic* is not very appealing. But the reason for this is not dissipation from political overexertion. There are passages in *Local Anaesthetic* that rank with the most dynamic in the earlier novels. If the nature of an episode demands the old anarchic gesture, Grass can supply it, as in this passage: "But no pain, only rage. He's doing it on purpose. . . . (My rage was looking for expression.) While Water Pik and my dentist were displaced by whole-wheat bread, the smell subsists: rage. While the large-sized dishwasher re-lieves the smiling housewife of work, my rage mounts and wants to smash built-in furniture. Rage that wants to slash Dunlop tires and use Mazda light bulbs for target practice. Rage rising from my smooth-wrinkled socks through both trouser legs and bunching above my well-hung parts. Pure rage. Fore-taste of rage that drowns out the aftertaste. Silenced rage. Rage silent to high heaven. (Never—though Vero Lewand has gone to great lengths to provoke me—has my junior class succeeded in putting me in such a rage.) Forty-year-old, stored-up, accumulated, cork-popping rage. It's got to come out. Ink rage. Rage unappeased by color, black and white hatching, layer on layer. Rage about and against everything. Brushstroke rage. Rage projects: bulldozers!"[7] That such passages are few and far between is the result of

---

6. Hellmuth Karasek, "Zahn gezogen," *Die Zeit*, September 6, 1969 (trans-lation mine).

7. Günter Grass, *Local Anaesthetic* (New York: A Helen and Kurt Wolff Book, Harcourt, Brace & World [1970]), pp. 123–124 (referred to in the text hereafter by page number); Günter Grass, *örtlich betäubt* (Neuwied: Luchter-hand, 1969), p. 158 (referred to hereafter in the notes by page number):
Aber kein Schmerz, nur Wut. Er macht das mit Absicht. . . . (Meine Wut suchte Ausdrücke.) Während Aqua-Pik und mein Zahnarzt vom Vollkornbrot verdrängt werden, riecht es immer noch: Wut. Auch während die große Geschirrspülmaschine der lachenden Hausfrau die Arbeit abnimmt, steigert sich Wut und will Einbaumöbel zertrümmern. Wut, die Dunlop-Reifen schlit-zen und Osram-Birnen abknallen will. Von den glattkrausen Socken durch beide Hosenbeine steigende, sich überm Gehänge bündelnde Wut. Artikellos Wut. Vorgeschmack Wut, der den Nachgeschmack Wut übertönt. Maulgesperrt Wut. Wut, die zum Himmel schweigt. (Nie hat mich meine 12a—so sehr Vero

choice on Grass's part. It is not the result of a sudden inability to produce them. The earlier novels in their refusal to ally themselves with any moral or social aims seem to me an extreme manifestation of what Lucien Goldmann calls the critical spirit in the dialectic of the modern novel.[8] The extreme complexity of Grass's earlier fiction is not set off by a unified world view, or, less sweepingly expressed, by a unifying, supra-individual value constant. There is in it only a critical, not a dogmatic element. In so far as these works direct themselves principally at the Nazi period, the predominance of the critical spirit is no doubt legitimate—at least to the non-Marxist view. Only if Grass returned once more to the war would it be admissible for him to continue in the vein of his earlier novels, for Grass now is a man who has given public assent to the fundamentals of the state in which he lives. He has rejected for himself the separation between artist and citizen. He has, in short, made a choice. His new novel is written in conformity with that choice. Hence the critical spirit cannot be as strong here as in his earlier fiction. In terms of form, there now has to be more restraint and a greater interest in ideas, particularly political ideas. In *Local Anaesthetic* there is a "new" Grass in the sense that he attempts to balance the critical with the dogmatic element. In *Local Anaesthetic* he aims to develop a dialectic unity in which a value constant serves to place all private problems and political tensions in perspective.

The plot of *Local Anaesthetic* is lean and has an economy of episode reminiscent of *Cat and Mouse,* even though the narrator is much more often the *raisonneur* than the *raconteur*. The localities are little more than props, just as the characters are, as it were, confined to a stage. In this respect it is especially noticeable that *Local Anaesthetic* is a twin to *Uptight*. In this novel Grass focuses on the characters as such, and not also on the locality. He does not allow his figures the shelter and sustenance a topography might give them. Therefore, they are much more vulnerable than those in his earlier fiction. Such exposure, however, must not be confused with weak characterization. Their vulnerability is essential to the theme of the novel.

In the first of three sections of the book Eberhard Starusch, a teacher in a West Berlin "Gymnasium," undertakes to have his teeth treated. Sitting in the chair, he listens to the dentist's ruminations about the history of den-

---

Lewand zu provozieren versuchte—in solche Wut bringen können.) Vierzigjährige, abgelagerte, gestaute, den Korken treibende Wut. Denn das muß raus. Die Tinte Wut. Von keiner Farbe besänftigt, schwarzweiß gestrichelt, Lage auf Lage Wut. Über gegen auf alles Wut. Der Pinselschlag Wut. Entwürfe der Wut: Bulldozer!

8. Lucien Goldmann, "Criticism and Dogmatism in Literature," in *To Free a Generation: The Dialectics of Liberation,* ed. David Cooper (New York: Collier, Macmillan, 1969), pp. 128–149.

tistry, pretends to be engaged in extensive dialogue with the dentist, and remembers his own past. As he does so, he blends it into the television picture which he is encouraged to watch to distract him from the pain. In Part II, recuperating from his ordeal, Starusch addresses himself to his favorite student, Scherbaum, who plans to burn his dog on the Kurfürstendamm in protest against the Vietnam war. Scherbaum changes his mind. In Part III, Starusch's dental treatment is continued. Again in a mixture of fact and fiction he invokes a series of versions of his past, involving mainly his alleged ex-fiancée, Linde, and her father, who had been a field marshal during the war and after his return from prison employed Starusch as an engineer in the cement industry. In re-living his past, Starusch gives vent to his frustrations and dreams of violence.

The novel is set in the West Berlin of January, 1967. The situation is volatile. It will explode in the student demonstrations that were to rock the city and West Germany for months. These tensions provide *Local Anaesthetic* with an unequivocal main theme, the first of Grass's novels to be focused in such a way. It is revealed by the nature of the main blocks of action, be they real or imaginary: Scherbaum plans to douse his dog with gasoline and set him afire; Starusch undergoes painful dental work; Starusch dreams of murdering his ex-fiancée; even after ten years of prison, the field marshal still wants to re-enact the battles he lost. The theme is violence and its correlative, pain. The topicality of the problem of violence almost goes without saying. The background of the novel is not merely the violence of West Berlin, but by connection with Scherbaum's intended protest, the violence of the world at large in terms of the Vietnam war, whose atrocities are subject to unprecedented exposure. To varying degrees it impinges on the life of every major figure in the book. As a teenager, Starusch had been the head of a band of young thugs who were against all and everything and were possibly responsible for the deaths of a number of navy cadets. For Scherbaum, his plan to burn the dog is obviously the major crisis of his young life. His girl, Veronika Lewand, who has graduated from picking emblems off cars to becoming a disciple of Mao, preaches revolution and prods Scherbaum to go through with his designs. Fräulein Seifert, Starusch's colleague and eventual fiancée, as a teenager had denounced a farmer to the Nazis for sabotaging defense efforts. She conceives of human progress in absolute terms, hoping fervently for the coming of a new world. In a sense the dentist, too, shares the problem. He insists on removing the tartar "radically" (152) and is a shade too eager to have everyone undergo treatment. Dental prophylaxis is for him the primary constituent in a grand design to solve the world's health problems. Violence is not only crucial for the world of Grass's novel but is a key to history as well. The historiography of torture which Grass builds into his book adds this dimension. In an effort to dissuade

Scherbaum, Starusch shows him a number of illustrations of human death by fire. Violence, then, is man's nature, and his universal state, pain.

The frequent allusions to Seneca serve as an approach to the province of pain. With the young Seneca who educated Nero and wrote his speeches Grass contrasts the old man turned sage who preached resignation in the face of tyranny. The common ground of resignation and tyranny as ways of life is the contempt for pain. It is viewed as dispensable to human existence. This is the crucial determinant of all doctrines of salvation, of all final solutions. The Nazi utopia of Starusch's past set out to conquer pain once and for all by eliminating all challengers. The utopia of the young radicals Starusch observes around him proposes to eliminate pain once and for all by annihilating the offensive social order. Essential to both utopias is the faith that through an act of supreme violence there will be end to pain. On the other hand, lack of belief in the possibility of a final solution, and a refusal to resign oneself to violence, to accept the mentality of the victim, leads to an affirmation of pain. Pain must be understood as an indispensable guardian against injury, as the warning signal of the apocalyptic violence of the utopian in all guises. Between the terror of a millennium of the past abhorred and a millennium of the future feared, Grass asserts the safety zone of pain. It is literally the beginning and the end of his novel. In the opening sentences Starusch tells his class that he is going to the dentist, and he solicits their sympathy. He hopes that the suffering he will have to endure will create an armistice. The book closes on the perenniality of pain: "Nothing lasts. There will always be pain" (284).[9] This is the dogmatic constant in the dialectic of Grass's novel. In pain as a value, Grass finds the unifying factor which structures the world of violence in *Local Anaesthetic*.

The argument for affirming pain is predicated on rejecting all doctrines of salvation and final solutions. Scherbaum's answer to Starusch's announcement of his forthcoming dental treatment authoritatively establishes the premise: "Your decision, tested in suffering, prompts us, your sympathetic students, to remind you of the martyrdom of St. Apollonia. In the year 250, during the reign of Emperor Decius, the poor thing was burned in Alexandria. Because the mob had previously pulled all her teeth with blacksmith's tongs, she became the patron saint of all those who suffer in their teeth and, unjustly so, of dentists as well" (3).[10] The torture Apollonia suffers is identical

9. P. 358: Nichts hält vor. Immer neue Schmerzen.
10. P. 7: Ihr leidgeprüfter Entschluß legt es uns, Ihren mitfühlenden Schülern nahe, Sie an das Martyrium der Heiligen Apollonia zu erinnern. Im Jahre 250, unter der Regierung des Kaisers Decius, wurde das gute Mädchen in Alexandria verbrannt. Weil die Meute ihr vorher mit Kneifzangen alle Zähne gezogen hatte, ist sie die Schutzheilige aller Zahnwehleidenden und ungerechterweise auch der Dentisten.

in essence to any torture committed for the sake of an idea. The suffering she undergoes is a form of therapeutic violence, much like the witch burnings Starusch shows Scherbaum to sensitize him to the horror of his dog's death. In the case of the witches the soul was to be saved from damnation by an act of absolute therapy. To those out of sympathy with schemes of salvation, the formula is absurd, the therapy is false. But in a sense Scherbaum shares the frame of mind that designed the formula. When he thinks that Apollonia should only be the patron saint of dental patients, and not of the dentists, he reveals that he has not yet understood pain as indispensable and violence in terms of value differentiations. The dentist is not a torturer; the pain he inflicts is the pain the patient has chosen. He is on the side of the sufferer, clearly not to save his soul, but to minimize pain. Viewing it as a warning signal of damage to the body, he has no wish to eliminate it altogether. He applies small corrective and preventive measures. Starusch is given the option of having his prognathic jaw corrected by surgical shortening of the jawbone or of modifying it by the crowning of his teeth. The dentist advises the latter.

For the first time, in detailed digressions into the history of dentistry, Grass makes an affirmative and largely non-parodistic attempt at presenting science and technology, But, unfortunately, dentistry cannot claim to represent science as a whole. The cement industry, of which Starusch talks a great deal in the book, supports both bunkers and houses, as the case may be. In fact, in connecting it with pollution, as Grass does, he points to the destructive aspects of science and technology. But the story of dentistry is a record of ever more effective deterrents against the violence of organic deterioration and brutality of treatment. As Starusch has to admit: "So much that is positive: successful root treatments, the removal of tartar, the correction of faulty articulation, preventive treatment at the preschool age, the repair and rescue of molars that had been given up for lost, the bridging of ugly gaps—and he is able to appease pain" (191).[11]

Grass's novel makes distinctions between admissible and inadmissible physical violence. The affirmation of pain is the criterion by which we judge. Violence is therapeutical so long as it does not permanently eliminate pain, so long as it respects pain as a guardian against physical injury or the deterioration that aging brings to the body. Though theoretically one must affirm pain, in practice, it is unacceptable. Therefore the anaesthetic. But to be compatible with admissible physical force, it has to be local and temporary.

---

11. P. 243: Allerlei Positives: geglückte Wurzelbehandlungen, Zahnsteinentfernungen, Korrekturen fehlerhafter Artikulation, vorbeugende Behandlung im vorschulischen Alter, das Ausbessern und Retten schon verloren geglaubter Backenzähne, Überbrückungen häßlicher Zahnlücken—und den Schmerz kann er beschwichtigen.

It must be confined to precise limits, so that the body can continue to remain sensitive and avoid accelerated physical deterioration. Only Vero Lewand, politically the most radical figure of the novel, rejects this notion. Only she thinks of treating Starusch's teeth in terms of extraction. The dentist is not interested in this solution: "The precipitate extraction of teeth, this mania for creating gaps that no longer hurt, is action without knowledge" (152).[12]

Sensitivity to pain also acts as a safeguard against psychic deterioration. Here, too, it is unacceptable. As Starusch has to take medication when his teeth trouble him, so too he has to find an anaesthetic for the anguish brought on by the memory of his ex-fiancée, Linde. The dentist tells Starusch: "[Your engagement is] a neurotic growth of hatred. Often it bursts into action years later (compensation)" (70).[13] In other words, Starusch uses the imagined murders of Linde to anaesthetize his psychic pain. But this is not enough. He must supplement the anaesthetic with curative measures that reach the origin of the injury. Starusch agitates against Scherbaum's plan and steers toward a new liaison with Fräulein Seifert. Therefore, his fantasies are to some degree successful. Primarily, Grass uses television to visualize the process the dentist describes. What appears on the screen seems monstrous, at first. Starusch projects various spectacular murders on it. The commercials stimulate him to conjure up bulldozers to rid the world of the avalanches of advertised goods. But this surrogate violence is capable of sublimating frustrations. Starusch's television murders, gross though they may be, are painkillers. This becomes especially clear in the light of an aspect of dental history the dentist tells Starusch about. In the mid-nineteenth century the patient was forced to hold his hand over a candle flame while his tooth was being extracted. The point was to alleviate the torture by "dividing" it, as it was called (71). This formula, repulsive though it may be, is physiologically sound. In sophisticated form it is still in use today. That is, in the shape of what Starusch calls the prick of the needle that administers the local anaesthetic. The process of anaesthetic "division" takes the shape of repetition in Starusch's fantasies. Since his variations of murder are progressively coupled with remedial efforts in his real life, he achieves a degree of therapy. As he repeats his imaginary crimes, the emphasis shifts from one aspect of the murder to another. At first he focuses on the escape after the crime and on the torment of the fugitive who in one version turns himself in because he cannot stand his toothache any longer. Later, he stresses the murder as such. In the end he becomes a great impresario of violence who performs his nefarious

---

12. P. 193: Das voreilige Ziehen der Zähne, dieser Wahn, eine nicht mehr schmerzende Lücke schaffen zu wollen, [ist] eine Tat ohne Erkenntnis.
13. P. 90: [Ihr Verlöbnis entwickelt sich] zur komplexhaften Haßwucherung. Oft wächst sie sich Jahre später zur Tätigkeit (Ersatzhandlung) aus.

activities with grandiose theatricality. He imagines himself at a seaside pool as the operator of a huge wave-making machine which he uses to drown Linde and her entire family in torrents of water. Having finished his job, he observes about himself: "Tired, partly satisfied, he packs up his books, goes to his room, tries to be sad" (283).[14]

On the other side of the coin, unsuccessful psychic therapy is symbolized by the field marshal's sandbox war, as inadmissible therapy on the physical level was indicated by Apollonia's torture. The field marshal's ersatz violence does not remedy defeat. Though he wages his battles to change past losses into victories, he merely suffers further defeats. Linde sees to that. The only indication of any remedial effect is the field marshal's sardonic announcement that he will carry his warfare into another arena, into politics.

In making Starusch an active and critical television viewer, Grass contrasts him with the general television audience. Starusch is atypical. Suffering in the dentist's chair, he rejects the appeals of the commercials and sees them as irritants. Television (and for that matter possibly the theater as well) becomes on the social plane the means for sensitizing the public to pain as a signal of danger. It is because of Starusch's pain and his subsequent reactions that we become aware of this beneficial function of television. Grass implies that television should irritate by pointing to social disorders and, further, should act as an anaesthetic while suggesting remedial measures. Since it fails to do the latter for Starusch, he proceeds to do it for himself. But since he has a strong radical streak in his personality, some measures he imagines are excessive. He means the bulldozers to sweep away the world commercialism once and for all. Needless to say, they do not succeed. The advertisements return to the screen. He is more successful when he takes less extreme steps and simply modifies a commercial. He neutralizes its offensiveness and at the same time achieves a degree of sublimation of his past anguish concerning Linde. On several occasions, he sees a supermarket-style freezer filled with food. In one instance, he changes the script of the advertisement by putting Linde into the freezer, who then rises out of it like a specter covered with frost and proclaims that her fiancé, Starusch, is an occupant of the freezer also. In this grotesquery, Starusch again uses mental theatrics to take the sting out of his tortured memories. Next to his teeth, the memory of Linde is what troubles Starusch most. He continually imagines himself in different situations with her. But Starusch is not interested in giving us the facts of what really happened. He is interested only in therapy for himself. As he imagines the variations of his life with Linde, his pain is divided, and brief periods of anaesthesia are created. As Starusch's pain is reduced, the

---

14. P. 358: Müde, teilweise befriedigt packt er seine Bücher zusammen, sucht er seine Kabine auf, bemüht er sich, traurig zu sein.

reader becomes aware of its importance in the novel. The multifarious events involving Linde in ever-changing context make up a phenomenology of pain. In *Uptight* the Linde episodes are missing. Hence its thematic structure is not as clear.

Starusch learns to value pain as an epistemological tool: "I regard pain as an instrument of knowledge, even though I don't bear up very well under toothache and reach for Arantil at the slightest pang" (192).[15] He realizes that he has been a failure; that is, he has lost Linde. His chief error was that he heeded her exhortation to stay out of the struggle between herself and her father. Though ludicrous, the sandbox battles are agonizing exercises in ferocity. But the young Starusch had not realized the painfulness of the situation as a harbinger of deterioration. He had not understood that Linde's obsession with defeating her father was an indication of decay. She had sold herself to Starusch's rival, Schlottau, and even to Starusch, her own fiancé, to procure information that would give her an advantage over the field marshal. Linde herself had expected Starusch to put an end to her curious version of parricide. Calling him a "superwashout" (12), she showed her contempt for him by offering him money to go away. Starusch offers no protest and resigns himself to his impotence. It is appropriate that he must resign his position as a pollution-control expert. He is not fit to keep it. With the money given him by Linde he studies to become a teacher, an occupation he thinks of as an extension of his youthful days as a gang leader. On several occasions the book hints at the kinship of violence and teaching. Seneca spawned Nero. Starusch prepared the soil for Scherbaum's plan. The identification of the two is even closer in Fräulein Seifert. By offering homesteads in the land of the spirit, the teacher may wind up peddling a never-never land. Fräulein Seifert longs for a promised land. Obsessed with the gesture of protest, she categorically denies the present and awaits the apocalypse. She encourages Scherbaum in his intentions, endowing them with chiliastic significance. Her worship of violence even becomes an aesthetics with her. She keeps an aquarium of exotic fish where death and cannibalism are the order of the day. She delights in suffering. She does not respect it as a warning signal of injury. So immersed is she in her revelries of guilt that on one occasion Starusch has to slap her to bring her to her senses.

Physical pain has a conscience more sensitive than the anguish of the mind. Grass makes this point repeatedly. In one instance Starusch bluntly tells Scherbaum that his toothache is more agonizing to him than the war in Vietnam: "But I must admit that this ache, this draft that always hits the

---

15. Pp. 244–245: Ich werte den Schmerz als Mittel der Erkenntnis, auch wenn ich Zahnschmerzen schlecht ertrage und schon beim leisesten Ziehen nach Arantil greife.

same nerve, this pain, which isn't even so bad, but which I can localize and which never stirs from the spot, affects me, shakes me and lays me bare more than the photographed pain of this world, which for all its enormity is abstract because it doesn't hit my nerve" (11).[16] Scherbaum learns quickly to accept this principle. During the rehearsal of the burning in front of the Hotel Kempinski, he visualizes the circumstances of his dog's death so keenly that he has to vomit. The horrors of the war do not have a similar effect on him. Those who encourage him to burn the dog have no concern for pain. To Vero Lewand the enterprise is attractive because it takes the important step from revolutionary theory to revolutionary practice. Furthermore, she gives no indication that the injuries Scherbaum is likely to suffer from enraged witnesses worry her.

Scherbaum's decision not to destroy his dog is the voice of the conscience of pain. He tells the dentist that he is abandoning his plan so that as a forty-year-old he will not be trapped by the actions of a seventeen-year-old, as Starusch is. The implication is that one act of violence paralyzes permanently: It pre-empts all meaningful future action. In this extreme concession to the dogmatism of pain, even more so than in being sickened in front of the Hotel Kempinski, Scherbaum reveals how young he still is. He thinks in terms that are quite as absolutist as Vero Lewand's. To her, violence redeems, to him, it condemns. For her, it is salvation, for him, a sin. Scherbaum, the physician-to-be, discovers that the dog's burning would be false therapy. In an abstract sense, it would lead to Scherbaum's permanent paralysis. To repeat here in negative terms the formula for a justified use of force: Nontherapeutic, here psychic, violence is violence which permanently eliminates pain as a guardian against deterioration. Scherbaum wants to preserve himself, which means he affirms pain, its sublimation, and its recurrence. Sublimation, however, cannot be merely an anaesthetic. While it is at work, real repairs must be undertaken. Failure to realize this leads to the resignation that had had such devastating results for Starusch. On the grounds of resignation the struggle against violence is admittedly hopeless. Since violence is inherent in the human condition, one must resign oneself to it, because to eradicate it would mean, in an absolute sense, to eradicate life. But since violence is nonetheless objectionable, treatment must not focus on the cause, for that would be destructive of life, but on the symptom, on pain. Since this argument denies the feasibility of repairing the effects of violence, pain is not

---

16. P. 17: Doch muß ich zugeben, daß mich dieses Ziehen, diese auf immer den gleichen Nerv gerichtete Zugluft, daß mich dieser zu lokalisierende, gar nicht mal schlimme, doch auf der Stelle tretende Schmerz mehr würfelt, trifft und bloßstellt als der fotografierte, unübersehbare und dennoch abstrakte, weil nicht meinen Nerv berührende Schmerz dieser Welt.

a signal of danger, but the danger itself. This is the logic of pessimism. This is the logic that advocates the permanent anaesthetic, or, *mutatis mutandis,* the hedonistic palliative. Submitting to violence is in the end the same as committing violence. The consequence is paralysis.

When Scherbaum accepts the editorship of his school paper, he sublimates his pain, anaesthetizing it in meaningful work. His first project is to take the year 1942 and trace and compare the activities of Kiesinger with those of a young resistance fighter who was executed. But pain resurfaces quickly as the school officials argue that an attack against Kiesinger must be balanced with an attack on Brandt. Scherbaum compromises, dropping the account of Kiesinger in his story. Starusch evaluates the compromise as further proof that Scherbaum has been broken. Starusch continues to be a secret lover of false therapy. In one part of his mind he had approved Scherbaum's plan to burn the dog. In his own past he had once advocated a similarly excessive solution to Linde's sexual blackmail of Schlottau by threatening to kill her. But Scherbaum's compromise is not a failure. He has not succumbed to either of the two extremes that continue to fascinate Starusch: He is not a violent activist nor is he a pessimistic victim of resignation. Though he cuts his story, there is a good chance that his point is still understood. When in a year politically as tense as 1967 he writes about a young resistance fighter, he implicitly writes about Brandt, and Brandt's youth necessarily suggests Kiesinger's.

In the sensitivity to pain as a value which Scherbaum and, to a lesser degree, Starusch develop, there are signs of hope. Succumbing to the critical otiosity of stepping out of the work of art, I would maintain that it is precisely the sensitivity to injury, the respect for pain that formulates the perspective for the rejection of a nuclear war. An atomic offensive strike, the argument usually runs, is impossible because massive retaliation would incur unacceptable injury. The perceptions in the novel obviously ask to be extended to life. The topicality of the theme of suffering and violence demands it; the knowledge of Grass's political involvement invites it. But outside the novel the terms in which these perceptions are stated are flat. They become higher banalities—though, admittedly, effective election propaganda. For if pain is affirmed, the temptation of resigning oneself to the status quo and to the field marshals and Kiesingers, the heirs to the millennium of terror, must be disavowed. Outside the novel the thematic terms are distortions, just as conversely, life is distorted in art. In an ingenious summary of the thematic configurations of *Local Anaesthetic,* Grass stresses this point and insists on establishing priorities of aesthetic judgment for his book. He talks of a painter, Möller, a Danzig resident of the early seventeenth century who was commissioned by the city to do a painting of the Last Judgment. Since the idea of Paradise bored him, he finished that part of the painting quickly. Purgatory and the trip to Hell, which he envisioned as a boat ride down the Mottlau

River, were much more to his taste. But Möller ran into trouble when he used a well-known whore as the model for Sin. After objections were raised by the city fathers, Möller compromised by putting the head of his fiancée, the burgomaster's daughter, on the body of Sin. To obscure this objectionable shift of identity, he compromised again and painted a glass bell over the face bearing features similar to those of Linde. This is the focal point of the painting: "Not around the body of the raftsman's daughter, but around the silly-pretty face of his betrothed, Möller placed a reflecting bell jar, which to this day asks a riddle: What is this delicate little face, rather goatlike in its narrowness and mystically blurred behind glass, doing on all that lusciously rounded flesh?" The answer follows, tongue in cheek, in a parenthetical remark: "(Just look at the reflections that bell jar can give off; it mirrors everything, everything—the world and its contradictions.)" Sin is unchanged and fully visible, but it has a different face which we must identify through the glass bell that becomes a prism for the whole world. Möller places all the city fathers into the boat to Hell, but once more makes a compromise by putting himself in the river. The allegory concludes with the comment: "With powerful arms he holds back the skiff, and as he does so looks at us: If it weren't for me, things would rapidly go downhill. The artist as savior. He helps sin to safety" (277).[17]

As Grass informs us in this mock allegory of the ways he preferred not to discuss the problems in his novel, we are once more made aware of the balances of the thematic structure. Yet more important, we learn that the eschatological implications belong primarily inside the confines of the book. Möller's Last Judgment is authentic only in the painting. The banalities of pain, whether expressed in the figures of a Vietnam body count or in an aspirin taken for a toothache, become eschatological in their significance only in the work of art.

Irony and distortion as in the allegory of the painter Möller or in the spoof of the dynamics of pain and sublimation in Brühsam's make-believe cooking lessons for the starved prisoners of war reveal that the thematic structure is to be understood principally as an aesthetic construct. Starusch's musings and lamentations occasionally lapse into falsetto. Fräulein Seifert is

---

17. Pp. 349–350: Möller malte nicht um den Leib des Flissackenkindes, doch um die hübsch dümmliche Larve seiner Verlobten eine reflektierende Glasglocke, die uns noch heute das Rätsel aufgibt: Was hat das zarte, eher ziegenhaft schmale und hinter dem Glas mystisch verschwimmende Köpfchen auf soviel griffig gerundetem Fleisch zu suchen? (Schauen Sie nur, welcher Reflexe die Glasglocke fähig ist: alles spiegelt sich, alles—die Welt und ihre Widersprüche.). . . . "Kräftig stemmt er sich gegen den Nachen und guckt dabei uns an: Wenn ich nicht wäre, ginge es prompt bergab.
Der Künstler als Retter. Er erhält uns die Sünde.

a caricature of herself. The dentist, with his relentless optimism and un-flinching common sense, asks us to color him sanctimonious. Scherbaum is a monument on which we are sorely tempted to place a wreath. Vero Lewand is punished for her radicalism by marrying a Canadian linguist. The chief metaphors—dentistry, television, and the sandbox war—are overwrought. In them and in the figures of the novel there is the same undeniable element of obnoxiousness present in the quaint grotesqueries of Möller's allegory. The style, though all in all much more restrained than in Grass's earlier fiction, is still a formidable brew. It is a conglomoration of blurbs from comics, film techniques, political jargon, ponderously formulated trivialities, and tritely dressed philosophemes. Again and again, the parenthetical re-marks seem to violate the sequentiality of the narrative texture. The dialogue and monologue on occasion irritate us as being the malapropos diction of drama. In short, the style is an exercise in sensitizing the reader to the the-matic structure of the novel. And so it does not speak to us in the plaintive tones of its characters' little aches and *Weltschmerz,* but in the abrasive timbres of Grass's style. It gets on our nerves; it is meant to.

In the light of Grass's compositional aims, if they indeed are what this essay suggests, *Local Anaesthetic* is impressive. That these aims are artisti-cally validated in the novel, as I believe they are, must evolve by critical con-sensus. Much of the disaffection with *Local Anaesthetic* in the reviews so far, it seems to me, is traceable to a lack of interest in "critical sympathy," the first and foremost demand Grass's novel makes on the reader.

THE POET'S DILEMMA: THE NARRATIVE WORLDS OF GÜNTER GRASS

RALPH FREEDMAN

1

THE POET AS NOVELIST INVITES HIS OWN IMPASSE BY VIRTUE OF HIS TRADE. Yet such is the burden of the modern novel that most writers have to endure this paradox between inward and outward projection, between imagery provoked by a symbolic psyche and the social or historical consciousness that determines it. Actually long before our time the organismic theories of Early Romanticism had rendered the ancient distinction between form and content obsolete: The worn image of the well-shaped bottle containing the wine of message had lost its impact. The modern novelist, far more even than most of his late-nineteenth-century predecessors, is also a poet whose shrewd view of the world is couched in imagery. Günter Grass is no exception. On the contrary: effacing boundaries between consciousness and objects is his métier, his special forte, his strength and his weakness alike. As in most modern art, a universe where relations among minds and between minds and worlds are no longer distinct, vision and meaning, the historical and the purely aesthetic sense merge with one another quite as much as do the contours of reality and illusion. To distort Marianne Moore's famous phrase—gardens and toads are both equally imaginary and real.

In choosing Grass's early novel, *Die Blechtrommel* (The Tin Drum, 1959) as our primary example, I do so with the particular object of illustrating the poet's impasse. Other works, especially *Hundejahre* (Dog Years), which is far more fluid, could have been chosen instead. But this novel is a brilliant and, in my view, most successful display of a writer's way of rendering—and in rendering solving—the poet's impasse as a novelist. For, Grass's own protestations to the contrary, it represents a broad cultural critique at the same time as it projects a highly individual, frequently internal vision. Not only is this novel a narrative of Europe's demise and its re-emergence with false values, it also describes its moral decay as a gigantic artistic image.

The plot and the narrative conditions of this famous novel hardly bear reiteration, but it would serve the distinction I would like to make to recall its social setting. To begin with, history, with which Grass compulsively infuses so much of the tissue of this book, is viewed from below. The major portions of the novel deal not with the promulgators of the historical condition but with its victims. The Matzeraths, whose family dominates most of the novel, are middle-class shop owners. They run a grocery store. Their food, play, love, work habits, their religion and politics all belong in the lower reaches of middle-class life. Their existence during the war, and the Nazi period, which Grass evokes with such great precision, is a panorama of routines interrupted only by routine communiqués from the front. Yet they are also insecure. Economically they exist perpetually on the margin of middle-class propriety. Ethnically, and this was especially important during the Nazi regime, they were conditioned by the dual heritage of the Danzig region, suspended between German and Polish cultures. These insecurities—and the perpetual longing for firm ground under their feet—Grass made into his novel's landscape, his fictional history, chiefly by expressing them through a constant interplay of the palpably historic and "real" and the transparently interior and "surreal." In this way the tension between poet and chronicler is absorbed by a preoccupation the more deeply ideological for its apparent detachment. On the one hand, Grass delivers a dense, thickly textured narrative—of a life secure on the surface yet most precarious underneath. On the other hand, this story (almost compulsively driven by the force of chronology) constantly interrupts itself. The narrative that leads us through seemingly paltry daily lives during a horrendous time in history is always punctuated by significant scenes, lengthily "surreal" moments which tend to express the narrative point as part of an inner life—not just that of any one person but of the world at large. They expose the interior tissue of history, its flow, its stoppages, its coagulating blood beneath the outer skin of recorded fact.

In the more significant first two-thirds of the novel, Grass chose the dwarf Oskar Matzerath as his point of view and mask to supply both the off-beat consciousness to reflect these moments and the picaresque actor to connect them with the narrative flow, suggesting derangement and stability alike. Indeed, by creating Oskar as both narrator and hero, he placed him—and the story in which he acts—beyond the historical narrative. Making him "surreal"—with his drumming and his glass-shattering voice, his transformation, after the war, into a full-grown albeit hunchbacked man—Grass remolded the most ordinary fictional base and rendered it as a grotesque form of poetry. For it is essentially Oskar's deformed and deforming eye which creates those long "privileged moments," those scenes that wrench life out of focus, and gives the thick social texture its interior meaning. Indeed, Oskar's mask, as that of actor and percipient alike, reflects the contours both of the firm public existence, suspended in the history of the day, and its psychic and moral disintegration. Each scene, therefore, is affected by the hero's deforming action and by his subtly distorting mind which constantly probes the slippery subsoil beneath a seemingly solid surface: the sight of the eels as a prelude to Oskar's mother's death. In this way, *The Tin Drum* can portray conditions from within and also render history as a form of consciousness.

Like Saul Bellow's Augie March (similarly insecure), Günter Grass's picaro Oskar Matzerath is made into the vehicle of a dual reflection: of a relentlessly rendered history of a culture and of its interior decay. And like Bellow, Grass had to find a proper balance between this inner world and that concrete reality which exists in the region (Chicago or Danzig) where people love and die. He therefore had to adapt not only the broad expanse of his imagination but also his individual techniques—his use of characters, of landscapes, of things, indeed his very language itself—to a set of conditions that would reflect both the inner and the outer world. The latter is rendered by a hero who has acted, who has lived in the world of events which he has observed and upon which he now comments in retrospect: as actor and chronicler of history. The former is projected by the perceiving, internalizing eye, which grasps events and objects in all their dimensions, which views, and in viewing deforms, the world it encounters and which renders a world beyond time that exists in the insecure flux, as well as in the perennial present, of immediate perception.

2

The poet's stance—which allows a projection beyond time—is determined by his ability to make experience part of the inner life and to fashion it as imagery. Poetic consciousness, therefore, is profoundly *idealistic* in a philosophical sense: Distances between mind and world are reduced to nonexistence, and narrative objectivity (based on such distances) is replaced by a formal or aesthetic objectivity in which both self and world are imaginatively rendered as a unit. The novelist's stance, on the other hand, is determined by distinct relations between self and world, between minds and objects. It is *realistic* in the philosophical as well as literary sense of the term. In the modern novel, peculiarly in the modern German novel with its heritage of *Wilhelm Meister* and Romanticism, and especially in the fiction of Günter Grass, these two positions are constantly juxtaposed. Worlds in these narratives are determined not only by settings however richly conceived but also by distinct imaginative constructions superimposed upon historical realities. In this way, for example, the hallucinatory, oppressive world of cosmic guilt is imposed, in Kafka, on the everyday world of a Trial, Thomas Mann's Leverkühn upon the image of Faust, and the face of quotidian, corrupt, fearful, and indifferent Central Europe upon the distorted persona of Oskar Matzerath.

For all the fabulous realism, the palpable, even oppressive photographic awareness of each scene—like that group of tremulous youngsters about to plunge from the high diving board as an image of a trial—even despite the dry factual tone, *The Tin Drum* is substantially a lyrical novel which seeks to come to terms with its author's historical obsession. Soon after its appearance, as early as 1963, the critic Marcel Reich-Ranicki described the poetic organization of the work:

> In many of its parts [Reich-Ranicki wrote in his *Deutsche Literatur in West und Ost*] *The Tin Drum* bursts with events. Nevertheless we are dealing with a lyrical novel. Grass's relationship to his surrounding world is clearly intuitive and emotional and—in the best sense of the word—artistic. He is not a critical analyst but a wide-eyed observer, a scout fired by curiosity, an original juggler whom the game stimulates with motifs and words. Most dominant in his prose are sense impressions. With dogged stubbornness, he tries to make totally present everything that can be seen and heard, smelled, tasted, and touched.[1]

Realism induced by vivid sensation, an intuitive and, finally, an artistic remolding of the external world—these are the elements that go into the making of lyrical form. Indeed, it would not be too difficult to cite those features in Grass's large novels—in *Dog Years* as well as in *The Tin Drum*—which appear to conform to the Romantic version of lyrical design as set forth, among others, by Friedrich Schlegel during the 1790s and especially in his path-breaking "Brief über den Roman" (1800). This is not to say that Grass is typically "Romantic" or that he used Friedrich Schlegel as a blueprint or even that he knew him particularly well. But it is to suggest that his work conforms to a large European tradition, especially in German fiction, which takes its root from the Romantic conception of the novel. This is particularly true of the tension between the so-called transcendental or spiritual vision and the historical or "real" "letter" of the work of art, indicating that both are combined in "Romantic" or "transcendental poetry" which in its most comprehensive form is identical with the novel.[2] Moreover,

1. *Deutsche Literatur in West und Ost* (Munich: Piper, 1963), p. 221.
2. Athenaeums-Fragment No. 238 and No. 116, in *Kritische Friedrich Schlegel Ausgabe,* volume II, *Charakteristiken und Kritiken I,* ed. Hans Eichner (Paderborn: Schöningh, 1967), 204; 182–183. "Brief über den Roman," in "Gespräch über die Poesie," *Kritische Friedrich Schlegel Ausgabe,* II, 335.

an ideal work, in such a view, should reflect simultaneously both producer and product; a perfect theory of the novel must be the novel itself. All of these statements indicate a mirroring of a "real" in a fictional persona, of a "real" in a remolded or poetized universe. The novel—the "Romantic book" —transcends specific realistic depiction, as perfected by the English novel, to encompass a world beyond space and time where Laura could converse with Shakespeare and Sancho Panza with Don Quixote.[3]

In Friedrich Schlegel's famous blueprint for the novel two prescriptions emerge as crucial determinants of a form which was to become the antithesis to the conventional novel as it had been developed since Defoe. The first, which focuses on the role of the poet, and his persona, is the elevation of confession to the most typical as well as most praiseworthy form of Romantic narrative. It describes the central task assigned to the poet, and his consciousness, as he mirrors himself in the work, reflecting and remolding everyday reality into a new "poetic" reality. In Grass's novel, it suggests one important aspect of Oskar's functioning—as though Don Quixote had ceased to act and had remained behind as a center of consciousness, refracting the book's texture through his peculiar eye as he tells its tale. In spite of, and partly perhaps because of, his dry ironic tone, Grass's hero (as both persona and narrator) achieves transformations in the nature of "reality" by creating a poetic picture—with his various transformations (into dwarf and hunchback), with his obsession with toy drums, etc., but especially with his multilayered consciousness that seems to transcend time and place through its lengthy expansions in depth within particular scenes which act as "privileged moments." Oskar, moreover, is fully aware of this dual role. When early on he receives the desired ream of "virgin" paper from his keeper Bruno, he muses about the different ways with which to begin the story of one's life and suggests a chronology that begins before his birth—with the lengthy dramatized vignette about the wide skirts of his maternal grandmother concealing the fugitive grandfather-to-be as she sat in a rain-swept potato field.

The second feature follows from the first. In addition to a discerning, seemingly inactive consciousness, the novel's episodic design we have mentioned is of crucial importance. Indeed, as in Friedrich Schlegel's prescriptions, so in Grass's novel, episodes are used as structural motifs. In this particular usage, Schlegel called them *arabesques,* or "witty portraits of play," a term he variously applied to the picture album that composes the novel and to the novel's total image.[4] These arabesques are made to form the peculiar substance of the book within the poet-mask's narrative. Reich-Ranicki pointed to this feature in *The Tin Drum,* too, when he wrote of Oskar's fascina-

3. Ibid., II, 337.
4. Ibid., II, 329 ff.

tion not with conflicts but with pictures. "What earthly thing in this world, what novel," writes Oskar in his famous chapter "Photo Album," what "can have the epic breadth of a photo album?"

Clearly, the narrative emerges in this manner—as a sequence of pictures which function as "privileged moments"—set within the steady chronological flow of public and private history. We need not recapitulate the entire endless string of scenes to observe this development—from the grotesque wide skirts of Grandmother Anna Bronski, to which we have referred, to the battle for the Polish Post Office at the beginning of the war, from the various family scenes during Oskar's Danzig childhood to the front-line sequences in Bebra's theater and the entry of the Russians that culminates in the ludicrous death of Oskar's father. All of these pictures function as part of a Sentimental Journey, a picture album of the soul, while at the same time they project a coherent sense of history as they mirror the movements of external life.

Various modes are used in this lyrical endeavor to interpose such extended "moments" in the narrative flow, although clearly satires and grotesques predominate. For example, the satiric imagination is at its height during the sequences of "pictures" collected in the chapter "In the Onion Cellar" where, after the war, well-heeled West German patrons pay a great deal of money to allow themselves the luxury of weeping by applying onions to their faces in a communal orgy. The tone is dryly narrative, and playfully understated, but the satiric meaning adds an interior depth to the historical picture of postwar German life. It renders feeling and the palpable awareness of the inability to feel. Equally pertinent, perhaps, are the sexual wooing scenes with Maria—those classic scenes in which the fifteen-year-old Oskar, still treated as if he were of preschool age, gently seduces the sixteen-year-old helper of his widowed father while at the same time seducing himself. This sequence of "pictures," too, is written in a detached, seemingly "objective" style, but the individual portraits are fraught both with internal explorations that elucidate the stunted male psyche of the protagonist and the corrupt passion of the girl, both of which are enlarged to become symptomatic of the family, the town, the world of their time with its flagrant enthusiasms. Simultaneously, they also function as an objective exploration of their world, yet another kind of meaning that projects the final entering of Maria as both a sacred and a desecrating act with all its religious connotations. But these passages also stand out by themselves—as "arabesques." On the one hand they form a hilariously imaginative, bawdy sequence, with the summer heat and the swimming pool, the wide bed and the fizz powder with which Oskar first manages to excite her, yet they are rendered obscurely uncomfortable by Oskar's peculiar status as both the child he is supposed to be and the full-grown male he actually is. Still, finally, the sequence remains a social comment, illuminating not only the theme of dubious paternity which pervades the book (Maria, with child, possibly begotten by the dwarfish son, quickly takes up with the father to protect herself and to become respectable), but also the profanation of the sacred on a more commonplace plane: the degradation of the beloved first to a housewife, then to a shopkeeper who is prosperous in the end and knows nothing of the past. The orgiastic atmosphere during the Nazi era is blotted out in the deliberate amnesia after the war. Such scenes, then, function both as imagery and as narrative moments within the texture of the novel and as aesthetically distinct portraits juxtaposing the sacred and the profane.

3

So far the questions we have raised have only dealt with one side of the impasse. As long as we assume *The Tin Drum* to be exclusively a lyrical novel and expose primarily its Romantic strain, we leave open the question of its essential *realism,* not only in the obvious literary sense, but especially in the philosophical meaning of the term to which I have referred, i.e., of projecting a differentiation between the mind—Grass's mind and Oskar's—and the objects about which it speaks. Clearly the two tasks—which we have identified respectively with that of the poet and the novelist—cannot be kept apart. For example, in the scenes following Oskar's role in the desecration of the church (sawing off the legs of Christ and the saints), the trial sequence is telescoped with a diving competition, simultaneously real and unreal, which is equally developed within the narrator-protagonist's mind and in the world at large. Oskar is weighed down not only by a consciousness which he displays on various levels of past and present but also by his way of manipulating reality as an observer with a deep sense of historical consequences. The "trial" scene just noted is followed almost immediately by the Russian occupation and by the creation of Oskar's guilt, his responsibility for his father's (or putative father's) death which serves as the pivot of the novel. At this moment, like Kleist's Michael Kohlhaas, Oskar has found the point beyond which simply living becomes a moral and metaphysical monstrosity. If, then, *The Tin Drum* turns into a fabulous enlargement of the real, this exaggeration carries with it, ironically, a return to the real. As Grass's use of language also shows, this juxtaposition of clearly etched sense impressions, of physical sickness combined with a whimsical tone, represents his major successful attempt to escape from the poet's dilemma.

But there is also another level on which Grass functions as a realist—in the literary sense—which is described by his historical consciousness. His novel is about Europe, about Danzig, about Germany, and later the Federal Republic, during and after the Second World War. Whatever his pronouncements, it palpably revolves around an historical awareness—the sense of a more than symbolic identity of the sickness of the human mind and of the world at large—which is developed as a vast panoramic view. Again, traditional lines are clearly marked, for there is only a thin demarcation between the panoramic novel of images produced by the poet's confessions or by his whimsical wit (as in Rousseau or Sterne or Diderot) and, on the other hand, the panoramic novel of events which depicts lives and manners. Even rather low-grade historical fiction, such as Gustav Freytag's *Die Ahnen* (The Forebears), can be seen as a Romantic novel turned inside out: a collective hero wandering through time and space appearing in many disguises throughout German history as he ascends in time (but not in space) from the Germanic past to the apex of bourgeois nineteenth-century nationalism. Language apart, the structures of Grass's first two novels suggest a similar identity between a realistic and an idealistic imagination. Like the heroes of *The Forebears,* Grass's seemingly composite narrator—consisting of the two Oskars of the book—reflects portions of historical time both in segments instantly experienced (the "arabesques") and as panoramic wholes. Again, although like every schoolboy Grass must have known some of the books of *The Forebears,* we need not assume that he used, of all people, Gustav Freytag. Yet this elementary comparison may not be entirely out of place. Grass's book remains drenched with history as a retelling of events from below to lend it a dramatic meaning. Moreover, we know that he also employed chronology pervasively, beginning in the late twenties (at the time of Oskar's birth which he so miraculously recalled) and culminating in postwar Germany. At the same time we saw how he set this chronology side by side with often grotesque, sometimes almost mythical experiences outside time. Usually it is the personal event and episode that would assume such larger proportions and would supply the "privileged moment" of added dimensions: History is viewed through the death of Oskar's mother, through Roswitha's calamity on the Western front, through the father's ludicrous death which fixes him in a state of guilt. Such impositions of the grotesque and symbolic upon the real may also remind the reader, more pertinently, of Thomas Mann, especially of *Doktor Faustus.* Yet whichever analogy we choose, it does not rest in a parallel with any particular writer but in a problem all of them share: the juxtaposition of an imaginative vision of time—of history as a whole caught by the symbolic imagination—with the empirical chronology recounted in the realm of fact. In the first instance we deal with the novelist as poet who creates Leverkühn as Faust and Schleppfuß as Mephisto, and who, in the case of Grass, projects Oskar, the sensitive, profoundly indifferent picaro, also as the image of a deformed and deforming heart symptomatic of Europe and Germany—victim and victimizer, passive and active alike. Here parricide may thus become whimsically gratuitous—the Party button with that open pin after all slipped from hand to hand like a quick succession of images. Indeed, as Oskar appears in the form of a child, yet is no child, he mirrors the social world and the world of contemporary history in their moral decline. In this way Grass connects, by means of his hero, the historical and ahistorical worlds of the novel. Like the original picaro, he acts and is acted upon, and like its Romantic descendent, he combines such a figure with that of a discerning consciousness that creates the tissue of the book.

If the hero, as both picaro and observer, represents one of the means whereby the writer's dual function as poet and novelist is brought into being, another is found in the overall *structure* of the book. Generally, of course, this structure follows a broad chronological movement. After the whimsical prelude, the narrative, we noted, focuses more and more on two phases of recent history which formed the substance of most of Grass's earlier work: the twenties, the Nazi period, and the War on the one hand, and the postwar disenchantment on the other. But by constantly bringing together the dwarf and the hunchback, the hunchback of present and past, by referring to his hero simultaneously in the first and third person singular, Grass releases different narrative universes which are put together in an intricate design. One of these remains chronology—the tale told by the thirty-year-old hunchback in the sanatorium. The other is acted out by that same narrator and consists of those significant moments which constitute the pattern of the "arabesques"; the world of Streetcar Line No. 9 juxtaposed with a dwarf's voice that can shatter glass, the personal murder of men and the impersonal murder of war—the artillery bombardments and the suicide of Sigismund Markus.

Still, neither the picaro's overt behavior nor the structural patterns he creates are wholly decisive in solving the discrepancy between the poet's "idealistic" conception of his world and the novelist's narrative world. Rather, the realistic panorama of Grass's work, directly front center stage, requires a particular language that can telescope the most evocative and the most clearly denotative prose and etch the contours of feeling with great precision. The same language will thus develop also interior dimensions, deliberately projecting mind into objects and visions into a world of historical events.

4

No one questions, of course, that Günter Grass is a linguistic virtuoso, or that a very similar attitude toward language, an attitude that uses words realistically yet by doing so expands their dimensions, does not pervade most if not all of his work. Using language denotatively increases the distance between the writer's consciousness and the objects he describes and manipulates. Using it suggestively decreases the distance as it heightens the intimacy between object and mind. Therefore, a writer who wishes to juxtapose the poet's idealisitc and the novelist's realistic stance must use both dimensions of words not only simultaneously (as do most poets and writers) but in well-designed modulations which relate to one another almost like musical compositions. Grass employs all aspects of words—allusions to childhood idiom, dialect phrases, wilful distortions of original meanings, and, finally, a kind of verve and motion that can be only barely identified with the actual narrator's speech.

Lyrical language, unlike lyrical design, is not an essential ingredient of lyrical fiction. Both André Gide's *L'Immoraliste* (The Immoralist) and his *Caves du Vatican* (Lafcadio's Adventures) are profoundly lyrical, yet the former contains many passages of lyrical prose and the latter few. Hermann Hesse's *Glasperlenspiel* (The Glass-Bead Game) is no less lyrical than *Demian,* whose language is intensely poetic, just because it affects the measured, seemingly denotative prose of the chronicle and the realistic *Bildungsroman.* Grass, too, seldom uses lyrical passages in the "purple prose" sense of the word. Rather, he develops a prose discourse (such as we find it prominently in Faulkner) which projects feelings and consciousness into things. The realistic world is established, yet implicit in its realism is a quality— sometimes ironic, often suggestive of unperceived depths yet always related to a consciousness behind the scene—that allows the reader to view both the narrative and the lyrical dimensions of the book.

A suitable example might be the epilogue to Oskar's father's death which uses objects—ants, even the lice on the Russian soldier which had passed into Oskar's hands along with a remembered phrase from Goethe—to give us a sense of dissolution (psychological as well as moral). The objects are all there, yet feeling and motion created by the language both enliven and at the same time deaden them as they convert things into events—personal, private, mental events to be generalized—while the objects themselves remain resolutely themselves.

> What strange things one does at the moments when fate puts on its act! While my presumptive father was swallowing the Party and dying, I, involuntarily and unaware of what I was doing, squashed between my fingers a louse I had just caught on the Kalmuck. Matzerath had fallen across the ant highway. The Ivans left the cellar by way of the stairs leading to the shop, taking with them a few packages of artificial honey. My Kalmuck went last, but he took no honey, for

he had to change the magazine of his tommy gun. The widow Greff
lay disheveled and undone between the margarine crates. Maria
clutched little Kurt to her as though to crush him. A phrase from
Goethe passed through my mind. The ants found themselves facing a
new situation but, undismayed by the detour, soon built a new highway round the doubled-up Matzerath; for the sugar that trickled out
of the burst sack had lost none of its sweetness while Marshal Rokos-
sovsky was occupying the city of Danzig.[5]

Clearly, there is in this passage no trace of "lyrical" language in the usual
sense, but we do note a subtle distortion of the perceived world as words are
shot through with feelings which of themselves they do not possess: the ants
and their "highway," the sugar, the honey, the widow a thing undone among
the crates.

It would seem that Günter Grass's linguistic universe, which relies so much
on descriptive words, pointing to things or impressions, conforms precisely to
a narrative world in which the surface of external events—their chronology,
their history—conceals an interior dimension. As in his narrative structures,
so in the texture of his language, Grass intertwines these two worlds, relying
on his words to indicate the things which at the same time are enlivened by
consciousness. In this special sense Grass's disavowal of "symbolism" is undoubtedly justified. For, like the Expressionists earlier in the century, he developed his internal (or "higher") dimension by projecting into the objects
of reality the motion and feelings of a poetic consciousness. "The incursion
of expressionistic lyricism into prose," to which Erich Kahler refers in his
comments on Georg Trakl's *Traum und Umnachtung* (Dream and Derangement, 1914),[6] took place precisely in this manner: Objects are animated and
set into motion as they become infused with the quality of mind. As words,
according to Kasimir Edschmid's Expressionistic Manifesto, function like
arrows piercing to the core of objects and revealing their "souls," so in Grass's
painstakingly precise yet fluid descriptions words reveal both their "core"
and their outer surfaces alike.[7] Poetic sensibility that infuses objects and the
realist's knowledge of their precise denotations together suggest both close-

5. *The Tin Drum*, trans. Ralph Manheim (New York: Pantheon [1961]),
pp. 394–395.
6. "Die Prosa des Expressionismus," in *Der deutsche Expressionismus, For-
men und Gestalten*, ed. Hans Steffen (Göttingen: Vandenhoeck & Ruprecht,
1965), p. 173.
7. "Über den dichterischen Expressionismus," (1917), in *Frühe Manifeste*,
ed. Kasimir Edschmid (Hamburg: Wegner, 1957), pp. 38–39. For a more detailed discussion of these points, see my essay "Refractory Visions: The Contours
of Literary Expressionism," *Contemporary Literature*, 10 (Winter, 1969), 54–74.

ness and distance between object and mind. In just this way, Grass's prose, with its seemingly factual, ironic tone, renders the things of his worlds in both their interior and exterior meanings. It is therefore not surprising that he has singled out Alfred Döblin as one of his significant masters.[8] Language describing things shot through with motion and thereby revealing their "souls" suggests the novelist's realistic and the poet's idealistic universe projected as an identical movement. Viewed, in verse, by a poet's eye, this simultaneous identity and separation of self and world is well expressed in the following lines from Klabund's lively poem "Ironic Landscape":

> Gleich einem Zuge grau zerlumpter Strolche
> Bedrohlich schwankend wie betrunkne Särge
> Gehn Abendwolken über jene Berge,
> In ihren Lumpen blitzen rote Sonnendolche.

With all its light-heartedness (and its suggested shadows), this is Expressionistic language at its best, written by a poet whose verse, and especially whose prose, shows several striking affinities with Grass's broad realism and with his highly sensitized, if often ironic, verse. Here, the opening line, likening evening clouds to rascals in gray rags swaying like drunken caskets, suggests several projections of things into minds and into the landscape achieved simply by rendering the objects—the objects in *motion* and in unexpected juxtapositions—without the usual metamorphosis of reality into that esoteric "symbolism" with which Grass has so often expressed his impatience.

This expressionistic manner of projecting consciousness into objects to render both the poet's and the novelist's worlds without recourse to overt symbolism links Grass's work, perhaps more than that of any other German writer, with that of a contemporary American novelist like Saul Bellow—incidentally also an author who has shown a great deal of impatience with "symbols." Although Grass writes in a different language, with very different convictions, from within a wholly different artistic environment, he shares with Bellow a need to solve the poet's problem as a novelist through carefully structured renditions of consciousness in which mind and language combine to play upon their objects. A description from Saul Bellow's *Adventures of Augie March*, which bears many resemblances to Grass's picaresque, might reveal certain linguistic contiguities as well. In the following passage, environment impresses itself upon Augie, who is molded by his

8. I am particularly indebted to Michael Hamburger for pointing to Grass's acknowledgment and elaboration of Döblin's importance to his work; see Günter Grass, "Über meinen Lehrer Döblin," *Akzente*, 14 (1967), 290 ff. For comparisons of *Die Blechtrommel* and Döblin's *Berlin Alexanderplatz*, see W. Gordon Cunliffe, *Günter Grass* (New York: Twayne, 1969), p. 57.

consciousness of it. In figurative language Bellow demonstrates the action of a universal world upon human consciousness of which it is also an emblem:

> Now there's a dark Westminster of time when a multitude of objects cannot be clear; they're too dense and there's an island rain, North Sea lightlessness, the vein of the Thames. That darkness in which resolutions have to be made—it isn't merely local; it's the same darkness that exists in the fiercest clearnesses of torrid Messina. And what about the coldness of the rain? That doesn't deheat the foolishness in its residence of the human face, nor take away deception nor change defects, but this rain is the emblem of the shared condition of all.[9]

This may seem different from the far less florid language of Grass, but the verve that sweeps minds into objects and turns landscapes into furniture of minds also exists in the latter's work. The following passage, this time not from *The Tin Drum* but from *Dog Years,* may suggest this particular bent of mind:

> So that's what they call the Rhine! Matern grew up by the Vistula. In recollection every Vistula is wider than every Rhine. And it's only because the Materns must always live by rivers—the everlasting parade of water gives them a sense of being alive— that we've undertaken this crusade to Cologne. But also because Matern has been here before. And because his forebears, the brothers Simon and Gregor Matern, always came back mostly to wreak vengeance with fire and sword: that was how Drehergasse and Petersiliengasse went up in flames, how Langgarten and St. Barbara's burned down in the east wind; well, in this place others have had ample opportunity to try out their lighters. There's not much kindling left. "I come to judge with a black dog and a list of names incised in my heart, spleen, and kidneys. THAT DEMAND TO BE CROSSED OFF.[10]

The language, the rendering of worlds in words, bridges the gap between the poet's fleeting images and the novelist's narrative design.

---

9. *The Adventures of Augie March* (New York: Viking, 1953), p. 201.
10. *Dog Years,* trans. Ralph Manheim (New York: A Helen and Kurt Wolff Book, Harcourt, Brace & World [1965]), p. 369.

5

Grass's situation is neither new to literature nor unique in our time. As critics like R. W. B. Lewis have accurately shown, the modern novel has inherited a peculiar position—a position which owes to German Romanticism, more recently to the symbolists and their followers, a comprehensive breadth transforming both the exterior and the interior meaning into a single image. Most modern novelists of note, then, are also poets who either absorb the world into their private universe or else project themselves and their minds into the world of people and events. Grass, like Bellow and others in America, like British novelists, such as William Golding, was moved to square his deeply lyrical sense with an obsessive historical or social consciousness. His ironies, his confessional tone, his episodic structure suggest that lyrical mode which was given voice by the pen and spirit of Friedrich Schlegel. But Grass's fierce historicism indicated his bent for a different kind of writing, one that sought to distinguish between minds and objects, between visions and events. Our examination of some of his stratagems in *The Tin Drum* may have shown how a lyrical structure, an expressionistic sense of language (a sense of language that turns idiomatic realism in on itself by using it for surreal ends) telescopes the poet's symbolic and the novelist's historic consciousness. Grass may well have seen himself chiefly as an architect creating monumental edifices for their own sake, but the bricks and mortar he used were supplied by a most urgent sense of the history of his age. In this way, the poet's dilemma has been dissolved in the thick narrative worlds of Günter Grass.

GRASS AND THE DENIAL OF DRAMA

W. G. CUNLIFFE

MUCH THAT IS POTENTIALLY "DRAMATIC" FALLS VICTIM IN GRASS'S WORKS to the derisive, even infantile point of view, first indicated in the short play *Beritten hin und zurück* (Rocking Back and Forth), later firmly established through the narrator Oskar in *The Tin Drum*. The tragic dilemma, the striking character in a striking situation, peripateia, suspense, pity, and fear are deliberately bungled while the narrator (with the author often plainly discernible behind him) prattles on about, say, teeth or ways of cooking fish. An instructive example of Grass's grotesque tomfoolery occurs at the end of the second book of *Dog Years*, "Love Letters." The scene is set in Hitler's Berlin headquarters during the closing phase of the Second World War. Hitler and his staff are depicted as spending their last days vainly attempting to trace a lost dog, issuing foggy Heideggerian communiqués to this end in a strange mixture of ontological and military jargon. Grass is plainly trivializing what is commonly regarded as a dramatic historical situation. The end of Hitler and the Third Reich, far from being a Götterdämmerung, is presented as an event of no special importance, devoid of drama.

In other words, Grass is engaged in a process which critics, borrowing from the theologian Rudolf Bultmann, sometimes call "demythologization."[1] If Hitler were made the center of events, instead of the dog to whom Grass repeatedly and expressly assigns this role in the novel, a dangerously exciting and misleading myth would have been created. An example of inadvertent myth-making occurs in the demonic God-seeking Auschwitz doctor of Rolf Hochhuth's *The Deputy*. Tolstoy, in *War and Peace*, develops a theory of history which removes Napoleon, and all other "great men," from their positions as leaders and makes them into puppets of history. Grass, without digressing into essays, not only denies historical figures their leading role but, with perfect consistency, takes the initiative away from human beings altogether and transfers it to the inanimate world with deflating, parodistic effect, hostile to drama. This effect is especially evident at the end of *Dog Years,* where all human activities, public and private, from love-making to

1. Rudolf Bultmann, "Neues Testament und Mythologie: das Problem der Entmytholisierung der neutestamentlichen Verkündigung," first published in 1941. A literary critic who uses the term is Kurt Lothar Tank, *Günter Grass* (Berlin: Colloquium Verlag, 1965).

politics, theology and manufacturing, are relegated to mechanical scarecrows situated in the Brauxel's mines under Western Germany. Furthermore, the mine is a traditional symbol of the irrational part of the mind, the source of the poet's material, so that the scarecrows inhabiting this dark realm become mere projections of the author. The reader is made aware of the creative process behind the narrative and this awareness robs the scarecrows of dramatic impact.

Grass's deliberate elimination of dramatic effects, however, is not achieved without a struggle. He is obviously fascinated by the history of Germany and of Danzig, while his lower-middle-class character portraits rival those of Raabe, Fontane, and Hans Fallada. He knows, however, that the poet must discipline himself, must deny drama and color and be content with drabness. This necessity is the subject of Grass's poem "Askese" (Askesis) in the volume *Gleisdreieck*. The cat, who acts as the narrator of the poem, recommends a repulsive diet of offal, very similar to that eaten by Tulla in *Dog Years* when she is mourning for her brother, a diet of old spleen and tough liver from a gray pot. The food is atonement for immoderation, just as Oskar's mother atoned for her excessive love toward Jan Bronski by means of a repulsive fish diet. To the cat, immoderation means all that is temptingly colorful and dramatic:

> Die Katze spricht.
> Was spricht die Katze denn?
> Du solltest die Marine streichen,
> die Kirschen, Mohn und Nasenbluten,
> auch jene Fahne sollst du streichen
> und Asche auf Geranien streun.

> . . . .

> The cat speaks.
> And what does the cat say?
> Thou shouldst scratch the navy out;
> cherries, poppy, bloody nose
> thou shalt scratch out, that flag as well,
> and daub geraniums with ash.[2]

2. The English translation is by Christopher Middleton in Günter Grass, *Selected Poems* (New York: A Helen and Kurt Wolff Book, Harcourt, Brace & World [1966]), p. 49.

Anything in excess of a sober matter-of-factness is evil. How evil, is indicated in the punning line "Du solltest die Marine streichen," which means "do away with the Navy" as well as "navy blue." The colorful, however attractive it is, can lead to war. The red objects which the cat will renounce range from cherries, which are pleasant, to bloody noses, which are ludicrous and painful. Asceticism is not easy or obviously desirable; on the contrary, it is ashes on geraniums.

In the political sphere this necessary "asceticism" has one very concrete aspect which emerges from Grass's political addresses of the 1965 election campaign. Germany should soberly reject any ambition to regain territories lost after the Second World War (including, of course, Grass's Danzig). But it is not only the older generations for whom crusading myths are unsuitable. The young, too, are compelled to swallow the sober dish of reality. The seventeen-year-old Scherbaum in *Davor* (Uptight) and *örtlich betäubt* (Local Anaesthetic) wisely refrains from burning his dog, and even the youthful revolutionary Vero Lewand marries a linguist, and a Canadian linguist at that.

The clash between the writer's natural inclination to depict dramatically, and his recognition that drama (in the broadest sense) means the confirmation of dangerous conventional myths, could have led to a creative deadlock. It is the struggle to overcome this deadlock that produces the characteristically modern grotesquery of Grass's style—the grotesque that Schlegel foresaw with misgiving as coming to dominate the literature of the future.[3] Many features of this grotesque style seem to be derived from the type of theater that Martin Esslin has termed "theater of the absurd," which austerely rejects conventional dramatic effects and, in doing so, depreciates human beings.[4]

Thus, Grass's anti-dramatic device of causing action to center around non-human entities is pure Theater of the Absurd. There are the dogs and scarecrows of *Dog Years*. In *The Tin Drum* and *Cat and Mouse* it is quite plainly things, inanimate objects, that exert a magical power over events: Wagenbach aptly calls the method "compulsion by objects."[5] The crowds on the Danzig Maiwiese dance to Oskar's drum and the Niobe figurehead extends its baleful influence through German history, right down to the fall of Danzig. Mahlke, in *Cat and Mouse*, is dominated by his neck ornaments;

3. Friedrich Schlegel, *Kritische Schriften,* ed. Wolfdietrich Rasch (Munich: Hanser, 1964), p. 149.
4. Martin Esslin, *The Theatre of the Absurd* (New York: Doubleday, 1969), p. 4.
5. Klaus Wagenbach, "Günter Grass," in *Schriftsteller der Gegenwart,* ed. Klaus Nonnemann (Olten: Walter Verlag, 1963), p. 124.

it is the medal that makes the hero. In the case of Oskar's father, Matzerath, it is a Nazi party badge that makes a martyr. He tries to swallow it when the Russians enter Danzig, but the object, comically self-willed, refuses to co-operate, with the result that Matzerath is shot by a nervous Russian. This is a clear example, one among many such, of an object dominating human activity without regard for the dramatic distinction between comedy and tragedy such as even tragi-comedy depends on. Objects overwhelm man, and concepts of character and conflict are abandoned. It recalls plays such as Eugène Ionesco's *Le nouveau locataire* (The New Tenant), in which furniture takes control, or *Les chaises* (The Chairs), in which chairs very satisfactorily replace guests, or Arthur Adamov's *Le ping-pong*.

Grass uses the inanimate world to blur the distinction between public and private spheres, with the result that both are trivialized and rendered undramatic. The deterioration of the German character under Hitler's rule is reflected, for example, in the gradual brutalization of the carpenter's dog Harras, who begins as an honest German shepherd and ends a bit of a bully after having sired Prinz, Hitler's pet. Similarly, the lemonade fizz powder on which a chapter of *The Tin Drum* is based, aptly links the private intimacies of adolescent love with the public political frenzies of the thirties. The effervescent powder plays a part in the love passages of Oskar and Maria, and at the same time provides an objective correlative for the heady, dangerous enthusiasms of the era. The historical connotations emerge clearly when Oskar tries to obtain this fizzy powder in postwar Western Germany, hoping to recall youthful ecstasies. An elderly shopkeeper tells him that it is no longer sold, and offers Coca Cola as a substitute. West German progress and Oskar's maturity are mingled and trivialized as the advance from lemonade powder to Coca Cola. In the latest novel, *Local Anaesthetic,* the unease of a whole generation is reflected in the persistent toothache suffered by an aging schoolteacher.

Grass entwines the self and the world in a constant flux that denies to psychological complications and conflicts any importance in the shaping of events. Consequently, he ostentatiously rejects dramatic development or clash of character. In *Dog Years* he sets up contrasting pairs of victim and persecutor, and then allows their relationship to dissolve in ambiguity. Both the vicious Tulla, with her aura of bone glue, and her far less beguiling victim, Jenny, are lost in obscurity by the end of the novel. The relationship between Walter Matern and his partly Jewish schoolfriend, Eddi Amsel, is something far more ambiguous that that of persecutor and victim. Oskar's mother in *The Tin Drum,* caught in a potentially dramatic situation, torn between husband and lover, dies incongruously of fish poisoning, whereby Grass throws away a range of dramatic possibilities.

The structure of Grass's novels, too, denies dramatic development. The first three novels place their narrators in postwar Germany, while many of the events narrated take place just before and during the Second World War. The novels then proceed by narrowing the gap between narrator's present and narrative time, but in each case the effort is in vain. Postwar Düsseldorf where Oskar settles bears a remarkable resemblance to prewar Danzig; there is even a similar eccentric character haunting the cemetery. Mahlke, the true knight of *Cat and Mouse*, is still absent from postwar Germany. *Dog Years* begins and ends in a welter of history. At the end and in the beginning, Matern throws Amsel's pocket-knife into the water. *The Tin Drum* begins and ends in a cramped, hygienic ward in a West German mental hospital (the ward *is* Western Germany) after a futile excursion through history. Here, then, is a further parallel with the Theater of the Absurd, this time with what Esslin terms its "circular structure." Thus Ionesco's *The Bald Soprano* ends with the opening phrases, and the tramps are still waiting at the end of Beckett's *Waiting for Godot*.

Grass uses the circular structure to take a sardonic glance at West Germany. At the end of *Dog Years* the captains of industry are back in business. But it is doubtful whether it is accurate to label Grass a "satirist" as Henry Hatfield did at the 1965 Texas symposium.[6] Grass stresses the puzzling and grotesque inconclusiveness of existence, whereas the satirist, like Swift, Karel Čapek, or George Orwell in *Animal Farm*, has an object in view, which he attacks by pretending that a grotesque situation is a normal one. Grass has no such distinct aim—he simply parodies human activities, even where, as in *Uptight* and *Local Anaesthetic,* he is presumably not hostile to them. Scherbaum's youthful revolt is parodied as a laughable scheme to burn a dog in public.

Grass's parody is all-embracing. He parodies not only human activities (the scarecrows) but a variety of literary forms—the *Entwicklungsroman,* the epistolary novel, the diary, the picaresque novel, even the detective story (at the end of *The Tin Drum*) and the Bible. The drama, too, is parodied when, for example, Oskar joins a troupe of traveling midgets—this event, in itself, is a parody of the theatrical education of Goethe's Wilhelm Meister. In 1944, with invasion imminent, the troupe is sent to the Normandy coast. One of the midgets, Kitty, sings a cabaret sketch celebrating the coziness and prosperity that await the survivors of the coming defeat. Kitty's song reflects the theme of the play *Hochwasser* (Flood). Catastrophe and "nor-

---

6. Henry Hatfield, "Günter Grass: The Artist as Satirist," in *The Contemporary Novel in German*, ed. Robert R. Heitner (Austin: University of Texas Press, 1967), pp. 115–134.

mal" life are seen following senselessly one after the other, mechanically and without regard for the requirements of good drama.

Another theatrical parody in *The Tin Drum* is significant, since it places drama on the same absurd footing as the rest of existence by using the device of the "theater within the theater." It occurs when Oskar returns to the Normandy front after the war with the former corporal Lankes. There he parodies the dramatic device of teichoscopy by standing on a concrete gun emplacement to report events offstage—the suicide of a nun whom Lankes has, Oskar imagines, seduced. This incident is imaginary in contrast to the "real" narrative reports of Corporal Lankes's war crime. He had, in fact, shot a group of nuns whom his officers saw wandering on the beach just before the invasion. Yet this striking incident has left no mark on Lankes, who remains his tough, competent self. There has been no remorse, no crisis or dramatic change, simply a grotesque, meaningless event. Now Oskar's imaginary report mixes, in Grass's characteristic manner, the creative consciousness with the "real" narrative of Lankes's adventures. This report is, however, in the same senseless category as reality. It is just another grotesque event conceived by the human imagination. The theater and, in fact, imaginative literature is included in the general formless chaos. Grass expresses this thought not infrequently through a kind of "theater within the theater" in his novels and plays. In *The Plebeians Rehearse the Uprising* Brecht's dialectical theater fails to impinge, to impose order on the revolt in the real world. In *Local Anaesthetic* the images that Starusch projects onto the dentist's television screen are indistinguishable from the other, "real" events.

Before he turned to the novel, Grass tried his hand at plays which show the same aversion to drama and even the same techniques as the novels. His first play, written in 1954, is a one-acter whose title, *Rocking Back and Forth*, already points to the undramatic circular structure that busily arrives nowhere. In its eccentric and inconsequential way, the play is, in fact, concerned with the theory of drama. It might well have been intended as an introduction to Grass's dramatic work, as it bears the subtitle "Ein Vorspiel auf dem Theater," a reference to the Prelude to the first part of Goethe's *Faust*. In Goethe's prelude, the Director opens and closes the discussion, which proceeds in an orderly fashion, with all three participants contributing well-chosen words. In Grass's parodistic prelude the Clown, seated on a rocking-horse, opens the proceedings, which are plagued by doubt and downright absurdity. As the other two, the Critic and the Playwright, seem to rely on the Clown for any inspiration, the rocking-horse must be regarded as a modern Pegasus. His refusal to dismount from it is the poet's persistence in his childish, non-dramatic perspective.

The Clown starts by complaining about the absence of categories; he is, he declares, no longer appreciated at the circus because ordinary people—his employers, for example—are more comic than he is. The Critic and the Playwright, who have been joined by the Actor, have no solutions to offer, except to suggest replacing the wooden horse by a motorcycle (one of them has seen Cocteau's film *Orphée.*) They waver uncertainly between comedy and tragedy, while the Critic, invoking Beckett, proposes a combination of the two with a touch of surrealism. They all insist, however, that the Clown should dismount from his highly undramatic rocking-horse; but he, equally determined to remain mounted, tries to distract them with nonsense talk.

Then the Playwright causes a bed to appear on the stage in which, he claims, his wife is lying. But the love interest, which has been literally dragged onto the scene, is not allowed to develop, and the Clown remains unseduced by dramatic possibilities, firmly seated on his horse. Thus the play proceeds to reject conventional plots (for example the love triangle) and symbols (Death as a rednosed comedian). The Clown is all for low comedy, a scene involving sweaty socks which the Critic rejects although the Playwright sees tragic possibilities.

The theater is put onto the stage, in the manner of Pirandello, to show that drama is impossible. The idea is witty, but Grass's disbelief in drama gives rise, not surprisingly, to a certain sluggishness that dogs Grass's drama, including *The Plebeians Rehearse the Uprising.*

Flood, the first of Grass's plays to be staged, adopts the suggestion embodied in *Rocking Back and Forth* and adorns the plot with a love triangle. Nobody is really alarmed at either the flood or the triangle because everyone (except the naïve, lovelorn young Henn) knows that catastrophe and normality alternate. Aunt Betty, placidly sewing sunshades while the waters rise, does not interfere with the social outcast Kongo's making love to a willing Jutta. With a complete absence of suspense the catastrophe ends, and the return of order is marked by the emergence of an official from a grandfather clock, representing the senseless mechanical motion of the world. Henn is the only character who considers creating a scene when Kongo's arrival threatens to displace him, but Kongo quickly dispels this by pushing him out onto the roof. When the water recedes the rats prepare to leave, realizing, with sturdy common sense, that more traditional behavior would be inappropriate. Henn, converted to undramatic reality, sulkily returns to a resigned Jutta.

In the next play, *Onkel, Onkel* (Mister, Mister, first version completed in 1956), autonomy and ambivalence of objects receive more attention than in *Flood.* Objects, especially the revolver, working the categories that have no relation to any recognized system of morality or immorality, prevent the murderer Bollin, a frustrated, systematic man, from proceeding from one murder to another. The children's song, of a type repeated in all the early plays, is the expression of a world where dramatic categories and other structures created by the intellect have no validity. The gamekeeper, trapped in a pit, refuses to respond as drama would require, but, like an automaton, sustains his role as a pedagogue and a nature lover. When the children who rescue him from Bollin appear, he is merely displeased at the disturbance and gives vent to his annoyance in a schoolmasterly cliché: "Oh, these city children! Maybe once a year they go to the zoo, and that's all they know about nature."[7] The murderer, the gamekeeper, and the widow go on playing their assigned roles in a preoccupied fashion, while the real control over events lies elsewhere, in a region represented by the self-willed revolver, the real protagonist.

The same disconcerting fact is the subject of Grass's next play *Noch zehn Minuten bis Buffalo* (Only Ten Minutes to Buffalo), written in 1957 and a great favorite with student theaters. The title is derived from Fontane's ballad "John Maynard" which is based on the Lake Erie steersman who remains at his post when fire breaks out on board his steamer. The earnest, heroic striving and simple drama of the ballad are transposed into pointlessness with two dilettante railwaymen at the controls of a steam locomotive rusty and immobile in an Alpine meadow. Drama is mocked when these two worry about the coal supply, rejoice at the approach of Buffalo, and wrestle on a swaying tender.

In *Die bösen Köche* (The Wicked Cooks), the first of Grass's plays to be performed in the United States, the same thing, the denial of drama, is treated with a heavier touch. The plot concerns two warring groups of cooks in quest of the secret recipe for a desirable but repulsive soup which is gray and tastes of ashes. Esslin points out the analogy between this soup and the Eucharist, an interpretation which is in keeping with the significance of repulsive brews of all kinds in Grass's work.[8]

The holder of the secret, Herbert Schymanski alias the Count, finds himself unable to communicate the secret: "I'm sorry. . . . I've told all of you often enough, it is not a recipe, it's an experience, a living knowledge, continuous change."[9] This play, then, states that no statement can be made. In the Berlin premiere of 1962 the Count wore a mask that suggested the face

---

7. The English translation is by Ralph Manheim in Günter Grass, *Four Plays* (New York: A Helen and Kurt Wolff Book, Harcourt, Brace & World [1967]), p. 115.

8. Esslin, p. 228.

9. The English translation is by A. Leslie Willson in Grass, *Four Plays*, p. 281.

of Grass. This created an absurd circular structure by making the incommunicable recipe correspond to the meaning of the play. The inadequacy of language is underlined by the choreographic element in which rival bands of cooks swarm across the stage competing with red-clad soldiers. The play hovers between ballet and drama, between tragedy and comedy, and between the childish and earnest aspects of persecution. Its ambiguity is emphasized by nonsense songs, such as "What could be sweeter than salt." The senseless movement of the opening scene recurs at the end, when the cooks start to run away after the murder-suicide of the Count and his wife Martha. "It has something to do with legs,"[10] one of them says. Futility, absurdity, and absence of drama have been amply, perhaps too amply, demonstrated, without the light touch of *Only Ten Minutes to Buffalo*. Marianne Kesting criticizes Grass for having expanded a notion into a five-act play by means of choreography and stage effects.[11] Grass has not since attempted the purely absurd vein, for he withdrew his next absurd play, *Zweiunddreißig Zähne* (Thirty-two Teeth), although the undramatic subject of teeth still haunts his poems and his latest play and novel.

For his most important play, *The Plebeians Rehearse the Uprising* (first performed and published in 1966), Grass chose a situation full of potential drama, that of revolt. But Grass's play is unlike others on this theme, in that it centers around inactivity. Its plot and its whole conception preclude development or real action. Brecht did not intervene in the uprising; the Director must remain similarly inactive in Grass's play. In each of the four acts, consequently, the plot threatens to grind to a halt despite attempts to inject movement and action. A building worker suddenly starts to tear up a cardboard portrait of Stalin, a delegation arrives and starts to hang the Director and his assistant (a strangely listless scene), an injured man is dragged onto the stage with the flag he has torn down from the Brandenburg Gate.

This last scene conceals an ironic point. Grass's Director, as he states in his Shakespeare-year essay in *Akzente*, is based on Brecht.[12] For the purposes of Grass's play Brecht is attempting, by means of the "dialectics of the

---

10. Ibid., p. 288.

11. Marianne Kesting, *Panorama des zeitgenössischen Theaters* (Munich: Piper, 1962), p. 254.

12. Günter Grass, "Vor- und Nachgeschichte der Tragödie des Coriolanus von Livius und Plutarch über Shakespeare bis zu Brecht und mir," *Akzente,* 11 (1964), 194–221; translated into English by Ralph Manheim in Günter Grass, *The Plebeians Rehearse the Uprising* (New York: A Helen and Kurt Wolff Book, Harcourt, Brace & World [1966]), pp. vii–xxxvi, under the title "The Prehistory and Posthistory of the Tragedy of *Coriolanus* from Livy and Plutarch via Shakespeare down to Brecht and Myself."

theater," to lend a sort of heroism and power to the cowardly plebes of Shakespeare's *Coriolanus*. He regards with contempt, however, the unrehearsed floundering (*ungeprobte Zappelei*) of the real plebes, who are in revolt against the work norms imposed by Communist rulers. Now, when the man with the flag appears on the stage, real life proves itself to be unamenable to his dialectics. Ironically enough traditional drama rescues the Director and Erwin when the rebels prepare to hang them. Erwin recites a variation of the parable of "the belly and the members" spoken by Menenius in Shakespeare's *Coriolanus,* and the rebels relent. The whole scene has the effect of a parody.

Chiefly the play is a demonstration of inconclusiveness—the drama inherent in the situation never comes to a head. The Director plays a series or roles, from the hardened revolutionary to Hamlet. But by the time he is ready to join the rebellion, it has been crushed. Even in *Uptight* and *Local Anaesthetic* the same inconclusiveness is cultivated. The seventeen-year-old never gets around to burning his dog—which in any case is a parody of a dramatic situation. In short, any dramatic situation calls forth the parodist in Grass, eager to deny the dangerous myth it might give rise to, to strew ashes on geraniums.

Grass does not distrust the lyric form as he distrusts drama. Often enough, it is true, the language of his poetry is hard, unfeeling, and metallic, and the images are fragmentary. Some poems read like cryptic jottings of motifs and ciphers that are more fully developed in the novels—thus "Musik im Freien" (Open Air Concert) and "Die Vogelscheuchen" (The Scarecrows). It is modern poetry as Marie Luise Kaschnitz describes it: "Language which once soared to praise thee, now contracts, sings no more in our vinegar mouths."[13] At times, however, Grass allows his verse to "sing." The childhood theme seems to occasion these bursts of simple, traditional lyricism, for example in an early poem "Drehorgeln kurz vor Ostern" about the street organs that used to appear in early spring when the poet was a child. They become an image of endangered childhood: "Hurdy-gurdies—hearts that always grow green too soon." Above all there is the poem "Kleckerburg," whose title refers to the castles that he built as a child with wet sand on the beaches of the Baltic coast. Again the idea underlying the image is one of endangered childhood, the impermanence of happiness and innocence:

> hier, wo ich meine ersten Schuhe
> zerlief, und als ich sprechen konnte,
> das Stottern lernte: Sand, klatschnaß,

---

13. Marie Luise Kaschnitz, *Neue Gedichte* (Hamburg: Claassen Verlag, 1957), p. 12; the translation is mine.

zum Kleckern, bis mein Kinder-Gral
sich gotisch türmte und zerfiel.
Das war knapp zwanzig Jahre nach Verdun

.   .   .   .

where I wore out the soles of my first pair
of shoes, and being old enough to speak
learned how to stammer: sand, all clammy
for making castles, until my childhood grail
gothically towered and collapsed.
That was some twenty years after Verdun[14]

Apparently Grass feels that there is no danger of dangerous revanchist myths arising from nostalgic childhood memories, even if these are culled from lost German territories.

It is, in fact, Grass's lyric gift that gives his inanimate creations the power to support his novels without the dramatic devices of tension, peripeteia, and so on.[15] The inhuman entities are described with an intimate knowledge which Robert Graves calls a mark of true poetry—often indeed with a child's clarity. Moreover, they are often strikingly appropriate as "objective correlatives," so that they acquire a strong parodistic force. In his latest works, *Uptight* and *Local Anaesthetic*, set in modern Berlin, Grass turns to the present. His method is less lyric as he departs from the childhood theme. The dentist's lore is not so intimately realized, is more obviously imposed to illustrate the theme. However, the grotesquesness that averts drama is still maintained.

14. The English translation is by Michael Hamburger in Günter Grass, *New Poems* (New York: A Helen and Kurt Wolff Book, Harcourt, Brace & World [1967]), p. 67.

15. Marcel Reich-Ranicki, *Deutsche Literatur in West und Ost* (Munich: Piper, 1963) points out the lyric nature of Grass's novels.

MORALIST AND JESTER:
THE POETRY OF GÜNTER GRASS

MICHAEL HAMBURGER

WHEN I ASK MYSELF WHAT MAKES GÜNTER GRASS SO OUTSTANDING A PHE-
nomenon as a poet, the first answer that occurs to me is: the circumstance
that he is so many other things as well, an outstanding novelist, playwright,
draftsman, politician, and cook. In an age of specialists such diversity of
interest and accomplishment could well be suspect, as indeed it is to some
of Günter Grass's critics. Yet the more one looks at Grass's diverse activities
the more clearly one sees that they all spring from the same source and center;
also, that the unfashionable diversity is inseparable from his achievement in
each of these, and other, fields, because the whole man moves together,
within the area of his dominant tensions and concerns. I am far from wanting
to claim that this area, in Günter Grass's case, is unlimited; but it is strikingly
and decisively larger than that of most other poets in our time, and that is
one reason why Günter Grass's poetry is so difficult to place in terms of
literary history, trends, and genres.

In the early nineteen-fifties, when Grass was writing the poems collected
in his first book, *Die Vorzüge der Windhühner,* Gottfried Benn was still advocating what he called "absolute poetry," "words assembled in a fascinating
way" and not subject to moral or social criteria. On the other hand, and on
the other side, Bertolt Brecht was still advocating a kind of poetry to be
judged by its moral and social usefulness. Benn's emphasis was on self-
expression, the enacting of inner states; Brecht's on the rendering of external
and communal realities. If we ask ourselves to which of these sides Günter
Grass belongs as a poet—and almost all the better poetry written by German
writers of Grass's generation follows a line of development that can be traced
back to that crucial divergence—we come up against one aspect of Grass's
capacity to embrace and balance extreme opposites. Shortly after the publication of *Die Vorzüge der Windhühner* Grass wrote three short prose pieces
which appeared in the periodical *Akzente* under the title "Der Inhalt als
Widerstand" (Content as Resistance), in which imagination and reality,
fantasy and observation, are treated not as alternatives but as the generators
of a necessary tension. The middle piece, a brief dramatic account of a walk
taken by two poets, Pempelfort and Krudewil, presents the extreme alternatives. Pempelfort is in the habit of stuffing himself with indigestible food

before going to bed, to induce nightmares and generate metaphors which he can jot down between fits of sleep; the quoted specimens of his poems place him in the line of development which includes German Expressionism and the Surrealism that was rediscovered by German poets after the war. Krudewil, on the other hand, wants to "knit a new Muse," who is "gray, mistrustful, and totally dreamless, a meticulous housewife." This homely and matter-of-fact Muse points to the practice of Brecht, who drew on dreams not for metaphors or images, but moralities. Grass's treatment of these two characters is good-humoredly and humorously impartial. Those who misunderstand Grass's moderation, and moderation generally, as either indifference or weakness, when it is the strength of those who don't lose their heads in a crisis, could regard this piece as an early instance of Grass's equivocation; but Grass would not have bothered to write the dialogue if he had not been deeply involved in the issues which it raises.

Before turning to Grass's poems I want to touch on one other prose piece, published nearly ten years later in the same periodical, when Grass had become a celebrated writer and a controversial public figure. It is the lecture "Vom mangelnden Selbstvertrauen der schreibenden Hofnarren unter Berücksichtigung nicht vorhandener Höfe" (On the Lack of Self-confidence among Writing Court Fools in View of Non-existent Courts). The very title, with its baroque and ironic identification of writers with court fools, was an affront to the solemn self-righteousness of the new radicals, who disapproved not only of Grass's incorrigible addiction to clowning in his verse and prose fiction but also of his commitment to a political party more evolutionary than revolutionary, a party guilty of moderation and compromise. What is more, Grass came out in favor of a position half-way between what the radicals understood by commitment—the subordination of art to political and social programs—and the essential demand of art itself for free play of the imagination, the freedom which Grass identifies with that of the court fool or jester. If a writer is worried about the state of affairs in his country and elsewhere, Grass argues—and there can be no doubt at all that Grass himself cares about it passionately—the best way to do something about it is the way of political action proper—the kind of action which Grass himself has undertaken on behalf of the political party which he supports. As for his writing, if it is imaginative writing, he should resist every kind of extraneous pressure that would transform it into a vehicle or weapon. "Poems admit of no compromises; but we live by compromises. Whoever can endure this tension every day of his life is a fool and changes the world."

In practice, of course—and in literature as much as in practical politics or in cooking—it isn't a matter of this or that, but a little more of this rather than a little more of that; not of imagination or reality, of clowning or didacticism, of commitment or non-commitment, but of a particular proportion in every instance that makes for rightness. Because he bears this in mind at all times, in everything to which he applies himself, Grass is not only an anti-specialist but an anti-ideologist. Even his theoretical pronouncements are nourished and sustained by his awareness of complexity, an awareness which he owes to first-hand experience. In his imaginative works, including his poems, the mixture has not remained constant. Just as in his prose fiction there has been a gradual shift away from subjective fantasy to observed realities, a shift paralleled in his plays, it is the first book of poems that shows Grass at his most exuberantly and uninhibitedly clownish. This is not to say that these early poems lack moral or metaphysical seriousness, but that the element of free play in them is more pronounced and more idiosyncratic than in the later poems, in which the clown has to defend his privilege of freedom, a special freedom begrudged to him by the moralist and the politician.

It has become something of a commonplace in Grass criticism to note that his imagination and invention are most prolific where he is closest to childhood experience, by which I mean both his own, as evoked in the more or less autobiographical sections of *The Tin Drum* and *Cat and Mouse* or in the more or less autobiographical poem "Kleckerburg," and childish modes of feeling, seeing, and behaving. Almost without exception the poems in Grass's first book owe their vigor and peculiarity to this mode of feeling, seeing, and behaving. These early poems enact primitive gestures and processes without regard for the distinctions which adult rationality imposes on the objects of perception. They have their being in a world without divisions or distinctions, full of magical substitutions and transformations. To speak of Surrealism in connection with those early poems tells us little about them, because they are as realistic as they are fantastic, with a realism that seems fantastic only because it is true to the polymorphous vision of childhood. As far as literary influences are concerned, Grass's early poems are far less closely related to the work of any Surrealist poet than to that of a Dadaist, Jean (or Hans) Arp, whose eye and ear had the same mischievous innocence, giving a grotesque twist to everyday objects and banal phrases. In his later, post-Dadaist work, Arp also adapted his unanchored images and metaphors to increasingly moral and social preoccupations, not to mention the metaphysical ones which, much like Grass, he had always combined with his comic zest.

Most of the poems in *Die Vorzüge der Windhühner* deal in unanchored images, like the "eleventh finger" which cannot be tied down to any particular plane of meaning or symbolism, but owes its genesis and function to a complex of largely personal associations. Such unanchored and floating images were also carried over into Grass's prose, especially in *The Tin Drum,*

and some of them had such obsessional power over Grass's imagination that
they recur with variations in his poems, prose narratives, plays, and drawings. (Dolls, nuns, cooks, and hens are a few of those I have in mind. In
many cases these, in turn, are associated with processes—such as flying, in
the case of nuns—which are even more important to Grass than the thing,
person, or animal itself.) The substitution practiced by Grass in these poems
also includes drastic synaesthesia, as in the many poems connected with
music, orchestras, musical instruments. Sounds are freely transposed into
visual impressions and vice versa, as in "Die Schule der Tenöre" (The School
for Tenors):

> Nimm den Lappen, wische den Mond fort,
> schreibe die Sonne, die andere Münze
> über den Himmel, die Schultafel.
> Setze dich dann.
> Dein Zeugnis wird gut sein,
> du wirst versetzt werden,
> eine neue, hellere Mütze tragen.
> Denn die Kreide hat recht
> und der Tenor der sie singt.
> Er wird den Samt entblättern,
> Efeu, Meterware der Nacht,
> Moos, ihren Unterton,
> jede Amsel wird er vertreiben.
>
> Den Bassisten, mauert ihn ein
> in seinem Gewölbe.
> Wer glaubt noch an Fässer
> in denen der Wein fällt?
> Ob Vogel oder Schrapnell,
> oder nur Summen bis es knackt,
> weil der Äther überfüllt ist
> mit Wochenend und Sommerfrische.
> Scheren, die in den Schneiderstuben
> das Lied von Frühling und Konfektion zwitschern, —
> hieran kein Beispiel.
>
> Die Brust heraus, bis der Wind seinen Umweg macht.
> Immer wieder Trompeten,
> spitzgedrehte Tüten voller silberner Zwiebeln.

Dann die Geduld.
Warten bis der Dame die Augen davonlaufen,
zwei unzufriedene Dienstmädchen.
Jetzt erst den Ton den die Gläser fürchten
und der Staub
der die Gesimmse verfolgt bis sie hinken.

Fischgräten, wer singt diese Zwischenräume,
den Mittag, mit Schilf gespießt?
Wie schön sang Else Fenske, als sie,
während der Sommerferien,
in großer Höhe daneben trat,
in einen stillen Gletscherspalt stürzte,
und nur ihr Schirmchen
und das hohe C zurückließ.

Das hohe C, die vielen Nebenflüsse des Mississippi,
der herrliche Atem,
der die Kuppeln erfand und den Beifall.
Vorhang, Vorhang, Vorhang.
Schnell, bevor der Leuchter nicht mehr klirren will,
bevor die Galerien knicken
und die Seide billig wird.
Vorhang, bevor du den Beifall begreifst.

. . . .

Take your duster, wipe away the moon,
write the sun, that other coin
across the sky, the blackboard.
Then take your seat.
Your report will be a good one,
you will go up one class,
wear a new, brighter cap.
For the chalk is in the right
and so is the tenor who sings it.
He will unroll the velvet,
ivy, yard-measured wares of night,
moss, its undertone,
every blackbird he'll drive away.

The bass—immure him
in his vault.

Who now believes in barrels
in which the wine-level falls?
Whether bird or shrapnel
or only a hum till it cracks
because the ether is overcrowded
with weekend and seaside resort.
Scissors which in the tailor's workshops
twitter the song of springtime and haute couture—
this is no example.

Puff out your chest, till the wind takes its devious way.
Trumpets again and again,
conical paper bags full of silver onions.
After that, patience.
Wait till the lady's eyes run away,
two dissatisfied skivvies.
Only now that tone which the glasses fear
and the dust
that pursues the ledges until they limp.

Fishbones, who will sing these gaps,
sing noon impaled with rushes?
How well did Elsie Fenner sing
when, in the summer vacation
at a great height she took a false step,
tumbled into a silent glacier crevasse
and left nothing behind but
her little parasol and the high C.

The high C, the many tributaries of the Mississippi,
the glorious breath
that invented cupolas and applause.
Curtain, curtain, curtain.
Quick, before the candelabrum refuses to jingle,
before the galleries droop
and silk becomes cheap.
Curtain, before you understand the applause.

I shall not attempt a lengthy interpretation of this poem which would amount to a translation of it into the terms of adult rationality—terms irrelevant to the poem, in any case. In my context it is enough to point out that its subject—or content, to link up with Grass's early contribution to poetics—is little more than a sequence of kinetic gestures, derived in the first place from a personal response to the singing of tenors, but proceeding by a series of free substitutions and transpositions. These substitutions and transpositions observe no distinctions between one order of experience and another, between aural and visual phenomena, between what is physically plausible and what is not. As in Surrealist writing, metaphor is autonomous; but, though one thing in the poem leads to another by associations that are astonishingly fluid, the poem is held together by an organization different from automatic writing in that the initial phenomenon is never quite left behind. Ingenuity and intellectual invention, too, are part of that organization, as in metaphysical or baroque poetry. Hence the wit, akin to the conceits of seventeenth-century poets, which is essential to Grass's art. Grass avails himself of the freedom of polymorphous childishness; but since he is not a child, and even his poems of innocence include the awareness of experience, wit serves him as a necessary mediator between the conscious and the sub-conscious reservoirs that feed his art. The association of the bass voice, for instance, with a cellar, hence with wine and, most appropriately, with a wine barrel or vat in which the level falls, is so elementary as to be easily followed by anyone who has not lost all access to the sub-rational levels of his own mind. The likening of a tenor voice to "conical paper bags full of silver onions" is a little more far-fetched, a little more ingenious, but just as convincing; and so is all the play on light and darkness, bright and somber sounds, leading to the dynamic analogy of cutting cloth, to scissors, tailors and haute couture. Grass is at his most clownishly farcical in the passage introducing the woman singer who takes a false step, yet even her plunge into the crevasse is consistent with the whole poem's trans-sensory dynamism.

But for the wit and the more ingenious allusions in poems like "The School for Tenors" they would belong to a realm of clown's and child's play which is amoral and asocial. Yet even in "The School for Tenors" satirical implications arise from references to historical phenomena like seaside resorts, shrapnel, and, above all, to audiences in an opera house. The very short, almost epigrammatic pieces in the same collection present Grass the moralist looking over the shoulder of the clown and child, not least incisively in "Familiär" (Family Matters), which has the additional irony of judging the adult world from a child's point of view—a device most characteristic of the man who was to write *The Tin Drum*, as well as later poems like "Advent." Incidentally, "Family Matters" reminds us that Grass, a writer who has been accused of obscenity, blasphemy, and every conceivable affront to the *bienpensants,* was brought up as a Roman Catholic:

In unserem Museum,—wir besuchen es jeden Sonntag,—
hat man eine neue Abteilung eröffnet.
Unsere abgetriebenen Kinder, blasse, ernsthafte Embryos,
sitzen dort in schlichten Gläsern
und sorgen sich um die Zukunft ihrer Eltern.

.   .   .   .

In our museum—we always go there on Sundays—
they have opened a new department.
Our aborted children, pale, serious embryos,
sit there in plain glass jars
and worry about their parents' future.

Here the gray, meticulous Muse of everyday matters seems to have taken over from the Muse of fantasy and dreams, as it was to do—up to a point—in Grass's second and third books of poems. Yet the epigrammatic and didactic impact is made through fantasy—as in some of Arp's later poems—not through a consequential literalness, as practiced by Brecht in short poems like the "Buckower Elegien" and by Brecht's many successors in West and East Germany. Very few of Grass's later poems are as exuberantly playful as most of those in his first collection; but just as the moralist was not wholly absent from the early poems, the clowning fantast and the polymorphous sensualist keep popping up in later poems seemingly dominated by political and social satire. The creative tension permits, and indeed demands, a good deal of movement in one direction; but it does not break.

In Grass's next collection, *Gleisdreieck*, it is the poems that touch on divided Berlin which give the clearest indication of how fantasy interlocks with minute observation in Grass's work. The elaborate documentation that preceded the writing of *The Tin Drum* is one instance of a development that can also be traced in the poems and the drawings, from the high degree of abstraction in the drawings done for *Die Vorzüge der Windhühner* to the grotesque magnification of realistic detail in the drawings done for *Gleisdreieck*, and on to the meticulous verisimilitude of the clenched hand reproduced on the cover of the third collection, *Ausgefragt*. Grass's growing involvement in politics is intimately bound up with that artistic development. The mainly personal and fantastic poem "Ausverkauf" (Sale) in *Gleisdreieck* contains this unmistakable allusion to East Berlin:

Während ich alles verkaufte,
enteigneten sie fünf oder sechs Straßen weiter
die besitzanzeigenden Fürwörter

und sägten den kleinen harmlosen Männern
den Schatten ab, den privaten.

          .   .   .   .

While I was selling it all,
five or six streets from here they expropriated
all the possessive pronouns
and sawed off the private shadows
of little innocuous men.

The underlying seriousness of Grass's clowning—as of all good clowning
—is even more evident in *Gleisdreieck* than in the earlier collection. Without
any loss of comic zest or invention Grass can now write existential parables
like "Im Ei" (In the Egg) or "Saturn," poems that take the greater risk of
being open to interpretation in terms other than those of pure zany fantasy.
One outstanding poem in *Gleisdreieck* has proved utterly untranslatable, because its effect depends on quadruple rhymes and on corresponding permuta-
tions of meaning for which only the vaguest equivalents can be found in
another language. Grass himself has a special liking for this poem, the sinister
nursery rhyme "Kinderlied," perhaps because it represents the most direct
and the most drastic fusion in all his poetry of innocence and experience. This
artistic fusion results from the confrontation of the freedom most precious
to Grass, the freedom of child's play which is also the court jester's preroga-
tive, with its polar opposite, the repression of individuality imposed by totalitarian political régimes.

Wer lacht hier, hat gelacht?
Hier hat sich's ausgelacht.
Wer hier lacht, macht Verdacht,
daß er aus Gründen lacht.

Wer weint hier, hat geweint?
Hier wird nicht mehr geweint.
Wer hier weint, der auch meint,
daß er aus Gründen weint.

Wer spricht hier, spricht und schweigt?
Wer schweigt, wird angezeigt.
Wer hier spricht, hat verschwiegen,
wo seine Gründe liegen.

Wer spielt hier, spielt im Sand?
Wer spielt muß an die Wand,
hat sich beim Spiel die Hand
gründlich verspielt, verbrannt.

Wer stirbt hier, ist gestorben?
Wer stirbt, ist abgeworben.
Wer hier stirbt, unverdorben
ist ohne Grund verstorben.

Laughing, weeping, talking, keeping silent, playing, and even dying are
the spontaneous and uncalculated actions to which totalitarian repression at-
tributes subversive political motives, drowning "the ceremony of innocence."
No other poem by Grass has the same combination of simplicity and intricacy,
extreme economy of means and extreme wealth of implication. Apart from
the taut syntactic structure and the rhyme scheme, the poem is untranslatable
because no single word in English has the familiar and horrible connotations
of a German word like "angezeigt"—reported to the police or other official
authority as being ideologically suspect—or "abgeworben"—the bureaucratic
counterpart to being excommunicated, blackballed, expelled, deprived of
civil rights, ceasing to exist as a member of a corporative and collective order
that has become omnipotent. The same applies to the line "Wer spielt muß
an die Wand," where "having to go to the wall" means summary execution.

It is characteristic of the state of West German literature in the late sixties
that Günter Grass's third collection of poems, *Ausgefragt*, gave rise to political controversies rather than to literary ones; and the collection does contain a relatively high proportion of poems that respond directly—perhaps
too directly in some cases—to political and topical issues. Some of them, like
"In Ohnmacht gefallen" (Powerless, with a Guitar), were bound to be read
as provocations or correctives aimed at the radical Left:

Wir lesen Napalm und stellen Napalm uns vor.
Da wir uns Napalm nicht vorstellen können,
lesen wir über Napalm, bis wir uns mehr
unter Napalm vorstellen können.
Jetzt protestieren wir gegen Napalm.
    Nach dem Frühstück, stumm,
    auf Fotos sehen wir, was Napalm vermag.
    Wir zeigen uns grobe Raster
    und sagen: Siehst du, Napalm.
    Das machen sie mit Napalm.

Bald wird es preiswerte Bildbände
mit besseren Fotos geben,
auf denen deutlicher wird,
was Napalm vermag.
Wir kauen Nägel und schreiben Proteste.
    Aber es gibt, so lesen wir,
    Schlimmeres als Napalm.
    Schnell protestieren wir gegen Schlimmeres.
    Unsere berechtigten Proteste, die wir jederzeit
    verfassen falten frankieren dürfen, schlagen zu Buch.
Ohnmacht, an Gummifassaden erprobt.
Ohnmacht legt Platten auf: ohnmächtige Songs.
Ohne Macht mit Guitarre.—
Aber feinmaschig und gelassen
wirkt sich draußen die Macht aus.

            .   .   .   .

We read napalm and imagine napalm.
Since we cannot imagine napalm
we read about napalm until
by napalm we can imagine more.
Now we protest against napalm.
    After breakfast, silent,
    we see in photographs what napalm can do.
    We show each other coarse screen prints
    and say: there you are, napalm.
    They do that with napalm.
Soon there'll be cheap picture books
with better photographs
which will show more clearly
what napalm can do.
We bite our nails and write protests.
    But, we read, there are
    worse things than napalm.
    Quickly we protest against worse things.
    Our well-founded protests, which at any time
    we may compose fold stamp, mount up.
Impotence, tried out on rubber façades.
Impotence puts records on: impotent songs.

Powerless, with a guitar.—
But outside, finely meshed
and composed, power has its way.

Compared with Grass's earlier poems this one gives little scope for play-fulness. An almost Brechtian literalness and austerity seem to contradict Grass's resolve to keep the court fool separate from the politically committed citizen. Yet I think it would be wrong to read this poem primarily as a polemic against the radicals. The gravity of its manner suggests that Grass is quarreling more with himself than with others, that he is rendering a pain-ful experience of his own. The old exuberance reasserts itself elsewhere in the same collection, even in thematically related poems like "Der Dampf-kessel-Effekt" (The Steam Boiler Effect) which *are* primarily polemical. As for the trilogy "Irgendwas machen" (Do Something), its center piece, "Die Schweinekopfsülze" (The Jellied Pig's Head), was clearly intended to be a sustained satirical analogy, but somehow the cook seems to take over from the political satirist, deriving so much pleasure from his recipe in its own right that the reader too is carried away from politics to the kitchen. Perhaps the happiest poem of all in *Ausgefragt*—happiest in two senses of the word—is "Advent," since it blends social satire with the freedom and zest which—in Grass's work—appertain to the world of childhood. Even here, and in the autobiographical poem "Kleckerburg," the tension has become extreme, because the amorality of childhood is at once re-enacted and judged in the light of mature social experience. "Advent," in fact, juxtaposes the war games of children and those both of their parents and of nations:

... wenn Onkel Dagobert wieder was Neues,
die Knusper-Kneißchen-Maschine
und ähnliche Mehrzweckwaffen Peng! auf den Markt wirft
bis eine Stunde später Rickerraffe ... Puff ... Plops!
der konventionelle, im Kinderzimmer lokalisierte Krieg
sich unorthodox hochschaukelt,
und die Eltern,
weil die Weihnachtseinkäufe
nur begrenzte Entspannung erlauben,
und Tick, Track und Trick,—
das sind Donald Ducks Neffen,—
wegen nichts Schild und Schwert vertauscht haben,
ihre gegenseitige, zweite und abgestufte,
ihre erweiterte Abschreckung aufgeben,
nur noch minimal flüstern, Bitteschön sagen ...

. . . .

... when Uncle Scrooge again throws something new,
the crackle and crunch machine
and suchlike all-purpose weapons Bang! onto the market
till an hour later Whizzbuzz ... Puff ... Plop!
conventional war, localized in the nursery,
unorthodoxly flares up
and our parents
because the Christmas shopping
permits only limited relaxation of tension
and Huey, Dewey, and Louie—
those are Donald Duck's nephews—
for no reason have swapped shields and swords,
give up their reciprocal, second
and gradual deterrant, only
minimally whisper now, and say please ...

Moral judgment does not become explicit in this poem, and the implicit judgment seems to be in favor of the children who plan a family "in which naughty is good and good naughty" rather than of the parents "who everywhere stand around and talk of getting children and getting rid of children." What is certain about the poem is that Grass's new realism has not denied him access to the imaginative freedom and verbal invention of his earlier work. About that realism—as evident in poems of personal experience like "Ehe" (Marriage) or "Vom Rest unterm Nagel" (Of the Residue under Our Nails) as in those touching on society and politics—there can be no doubt, and even in politics it is realism that Grass opposes to the utopianism of the Left-wing and Right-wing radicals.

Whatever Günter Grass may do next—and he is the most unpredictable of artists—his third book of poems points to a widening awareness; and this means that he is unlikely to take his realism and literalness beyond a certain point. His involvement in the practical business of politics has imposed a very perceptible strain on him, but his essentially unpuritanical temper has ensured that the creative tension between innocence and experience, spontaneity and self-discipline is always maintained. Another way of putting it is that, unlike the ideologists and radicals, Grass does not want to carry politics over into private life or into those artistic processes which have to do with personality. If *Ausgefragt* is dominated by public concerns, it also contains this short poem, "Falsche Schönheit" (Wrong Beauty):

Diese Stille,
    also der abseits in sich verbißne Verkehr,
        gefällt mir,
und dieses Hammelkotelett,
    wenn es auch kalt mittlerweile und talgig,
        schmeckt mir,
das Leben,
    ich meine die Spanne seit gestern bis Montag früh,
        macht wieder Spaß:
ich lache über Teltower Rübchen,
unser Meerschweinchen erinnert mich rosa,
Heiterkeit will meinen Tisch überschwemmen,
und ein Gedanke,
    immerhin ein Gedanke,
        geht ohne Hefe auf;
           und ich freue mich,
               weil er falsch ist und schön.

.   .   .   .

This quiet,
    that is, the traffic some way off, its teeth stuck into itself,
        pleases me,
and this lamb cutlet,
    though cold by now and greasy,
        tastes good,
life,
    I mean the period from yesterday to Monday morning,
        is fun again:
I laugh at the dish of parsnips,
our guinea pig pinkly reminds me,
cheerfulness threatens to flood my table,
and an idea,
    an idea of sorts,
        rises without yeast;
           and I'm happy
               because it is wrong and beautiful.

Ideas that make one happy because they are "wrong and beautiful" have no place in the austere post-Brechtian verse written by so many West and East German poets in the nineteen-sixties. When he wants to be, Grass can be as realistic as they are; but the court jester's freedom includes the right to be fantastic, playful, and grotesque.

Grass's insistence on this freedom has a special importance against the background of a general crisis in West German literature, precipitated by its increasing politicization. While East German poets like Wolf Biermann and Reiner Kunze have been defending the individual against encroachments on his privacy on the part of an all-powerful collective, or of an all-powerful bureaucracy that claims to represent the collective, many West German writers have done their best to deprive themselves of such personal liberty as they enjoy. In extreme cases, like that of Hans Magnus Enzensberger, the conflict between social conscience and personal inclination has led to a virtual renunciation of imaginative writing. Those who have followed critical opinion in West Germany over the years will be familiar with statements about what can no longer be written: love poems, because love is a form of bourgeois self-indulgence; nature poems, because we live in a technological age; confessional poems, or poems of personal experience, because they are poems of personal experience; moon poems, because, as Peter Rühmkorf suggested well before the first moon-landing, astronauts are better qualified to deal with the moon than poets. Needless to say, all those kinds of poems have continued to be written, even if they have been written in new ways. Yet the fact remains that a great many people have been busy restricting the range of poetry. To be fair to them, there is some truth in most of their arguments, and a certain excitement is generated by discoveries of what one can no longer do. What is dangerous is to be dogmatic about it or to persuade oneself that one mustn't write this or that kind of poem because it has become anachronistic. If all poetry is an anachronism—and it was felt to be that as long ago as the early stages of the Industrial Revolution—so is almost every other human activity and the human species itself. Günter Grass's court jester at a non-existent court is undoubtedly an anachronism; but perhaps it is wise at present not to be thrown into a panic by that word, since the more we panic, the more we accelerate the process of obsolescence.

Günter Grass, in any case, has not worried too much about what can and cannot be written, according to the latest theoretical appraisal of the state of civilization. He has written what he was impelled to write, with a prodigal energy which—even in poems—has involved the risk of error, of tactlessness, of "wrong beauty," of bad taste. It remains to be seen whether Günter Grass can maintain his energy and spontaneity as a poet not only in the teeth of the ideological constrictors, to whom he has made no concessions, but also as he moves farther and farther away from childhood and the peculiar imaginative sources of his art. Since there is a limit to the fruitful tension between the politician and the clown, or between any kind of arduous practical involvement and the state of openness which poetry demands, it is my hope that conditions in Germany will soon make it unnecessary for Grass to assume responsibilities that ought to be borne by persons without his unique talents as a writer and artist. The tension, as I have tried to show, was there from the first, even when the clown seemed to have it all his way, and the moralist in Grass had not yet involved him in party politics. There is no reason why it should cease if my hope is fulfilled, since in poets practical experience is transmuted into awareness, and innocence is never lost, but renews itself within the awareness.

A SHORT BIBLIOGRAPHY OF GÜNTER GRASS

Die Vorzüge der Windhühner. Neuwied: Luchterhand, 1956.
Die Blechtrommel. Neuwied: Luchterhand, 1959.
O Susanna, ein Jazz-Bilderbuch, with Horst Geldmacher. Cologne: Kiepenheuer & Witsch, 1959.
Gleisdreieck. Neuwied: Luchterhand, 1960.
Katz und Maus. Neuwied: Luchterhand, 1961.
Hochwasser. Frankfurt/Main: edition suhrkamp, 1963.
Hundejahre. Neuwied: Luchterhand, 1963.
Die Ballerina. Berlin: Friedenauer Presse, 1963 (limited edition); 1965 (edition of 500 copies).
Was ist des Deutschen Vaterland? Neuwied: Luchterhand, 1965.
Loblied auf Willy. Neuwied: Luchterhand, 1965.
Es steht zur Wahl. Neuwied: Luchterhand, 1965.
Ich klage an. Neuwied: Luchterhand, 1965.
Des Kaisers neue Kleider. Neuwied: Luchterhand, 1965.
Onkel, Onkel. Berlin: Verlag Klaus Wagenbach, 1965.
Die Plebejer proben den Aufstand. Neuwied: Luchterhand, 1966.
Ausgefragt. Neuwied: Luchterhand, 1967.
Über das Selbstverständliche. Neuwied: Luchterhand, 1968.
Über meinen Lehrer Döblin und andere Vorträge. Berlin: Literarisches Colloquium, 1968.
örtlich betäubt. Neuwied: Luchterhand, 1969.
Theaterspiele. Neuwied: Luchterhand, 1970.

WORKS IN ENGLISH TRANSLATION

The Tin Drum, trans. Ralph Manheim. New York: Pantheon Books, 1962.
Cat and Mouse, trans. Ralph Manheim. New York: A Helen and Kurt Wolff Book, Harcourt, Brace & World, 1963.
Dog Years, trans. Ralph Manheim. New York: A Helen and Kurt Wolff Book, Harcourt, Brace & World, 1965.
Selected Poems, trans. Michael Hamburger and Christopher Middleton. New York: A Helen and Kurt Wolff Book, Harcourt, Brace & World, 1966.
The Plebeians Rehearse the Uprising, trans. Ralph Manheim. New York: A Helen and Kurt Wolff Book, Harcourt, Brace & World, 1966.
Four Plays [Flood; Mister, Mister; Only Ten Minutes to Buffalo, trans. Ralph Manheim; The Wicked Cooks, trans. A. Leslie Willson]. New York: A Helen and Kurt Wolff Book, Harcourt, Brace & World, 1967.
Speak Out! trans. Ralph Manheim. New York: A Helen and Kurt Wolff Book, Harcourt, Brace & World, 1967.
New Poems, trans. Michael Hamburger. New York: A Helen and Kurt Wolff Book, Harcourt, Brace & World, 1968.
Local Anaesthetic, trans. Ralph Manheim. New York: A Helen and Kurt Wolff Book, Harcourt, Brace & World, 1970.

AUTHORS AND TRANSLATORS

W. GORDON CUNLIFFE is an associate professor of German at the University of Wisconsin at Madison. He studied in London and in Hamburg, and worked for several years as a translator and interpreter in Germany and Luxembourg. Among his publications are two articles as well as a Twayne Series monograph on Günter Grass, an article on Max Frisch, and some twenty essays on British and American poetry and fiction for three volumes of the *Insight* series published in Frankfurt am Main.

RALPH FREEDMAN was born in Hamburg and spent his early years in Germany before emigrating to England in 1939 and to the United States the following year. Freedman received his B.A. degree from the University of Washington in 1948, his M.A. from Brown University in 1950, and his Ph.D. in comparative literature from Yale University in 1954. He has taught at Rutgers University and at the Universities of Iowa, Washington, and Wisconsin. He is now professor of comparative literature at Princeton University. Freedman has numerous publications in the field of comparative studies on such writers as Nathaniel Hawthorne and Conrad Ferdinand Meyer, Wallace Stevens and Rainer Maria Rilke, Coleridge and Novalis. He is the author of *The Lyrical Novel* (1963).

ERHARD FRIEDRICHSMEYER was born in Rugby, North Dakota. After graduating from Lakeland College in 1958 he continued his studies at the University of Wisconsin, receiving the M.A. in 1959 and the Ph.D. in 1964. Friedrichsmeyer has taught at Concordia College (Moorhead, Minnesota) and at the Universities of Minnesota and Wisconsin at Milwaukee. He is now professor at the University of Cincinnati, on leave as director of the National Work Study Program at Schloß Gracht in Liblar, Germany. Among his publications are articles on Günter Grass, Uwe Johnson, and Peter Weiss.

GÜNTER GRASS, born in Danzig in 1927, was catapulted from obscurity to international prominence with the publication of *Die Blechtrommel* (The Tin Drum) in 1959. While still in his teens he had served briefly in an anti-aircraft battery, and after two years of American captivity had made his way down the Rhine from Bavaria to Düsseldorf, where he apprenticed himself to a tombstone cutter in order to earn money for art school. Subsequently he studied sculpture and graphic art in Düsseldorf and Berlin. His first literary efforts were lyric poems, which his wife—a former ballerina in Switzerland—encouraged him to write. He first read before the Group 47 in 1955, and in 1958 won the Group Prize for excerpts from the budding narrative of Oskar Matzerath. Until the last meeting of the Group 47 in 1967, Grass continued to participate, not only giving readings on occasion but contributing a critical voice which won instant recognition for its perceptivity and fairness. Denied the Bremen Literary Prize in 1960 when offended citizens overruled the prize jury, Grass received the Berlin

Critics' Award nevertheless, followed in 1962 by the French "Le meilleur livre étranger," in 1965 by the Georg Büchner Prize, and in 1968 by the Theodor Fontane Prize. Through the productive literary years (see the bibliography of his publications above) he has not neglected his art: He has designed the dust jackets for his books and has illustrated his volumes of poetry, the Wagenbach edition of *Onkel, Onkel,* and the books of selected friends. He has aroused spirited attacks from the extremes of Left and Right political groups because of his middle-of-the-road stance in exuberant political support of the Socialist Party and its leader, his friend Willy Brandt, now the chancellor of the Federal Republic of Germany, formerly mayor of West Berlin. Grass lives there now, with his wife and four children.

MICHAEL HAMBURGER, a highly respected translator not only of Günter Grass's lyric poetry but also of Friedrich Hölderlin and a host of modern German poets, was born in Berlin and educated in England. He not only is a translator but is a poet himself, as well as a critic and teacher. He has taught in England at the University College, London, and the University of Reading. In the United States he has held guest positions at Mount Holyoke and the State University of New York at Buffalo. In the fall of 1970 he will be a visiting fellow at the Center for Humanities at Wesleyan University (Connecticut) and in the spring of 1971 will hold a professorship at the State University of New York at Stony Brook. Hamburger has been the recipient of a Bollingen Foundation Fellowship and has received awards in recognition of the excellence of his translations, including the German Academy of Language and Literature in Darmstadt (1962) and the Arts Council of Great Britain (1969). His books of literary criticism are *Reason and Energy* (1957), *From Prophecy to Exorcism* (1965), and *The Truth of Poetry* (1970). His volumes of poetry are *Flowering Cactus* (1950), *Poems 1950–1951* (1952), *The Dual Site* (1958), and *Travelling* (1969). His translations have appeared in numerous anthologies and literary journals.

A. LESLIE WILLSON, the editor of DIMENSION and a professor of German at The University of Texas at Austin, has published a monograph study of German Romantic involvement with Indic myth, numerous studies of German Romanticism and of modern German authors, and most recently a comparative study of contemporary surrealist tendencies demonstrated by German authors and the American author Donald Barthelme. With the cooperation of Ninon Tallon Karlweis, Grass's dramatic agent, Willson arranged for the production of a miscellany of poetry, narrative, and drama by Günter Grass in a premiere production at The Pennsylvania State University in February, 1966, under the title "An Album of Günter Grass." In addition to acting as literary advisor for the presentation, Willson translated the poems recited by "The Poet." The show, under the title "The World of Günter Grass," opened in April, 1966, at The Pocket Theater off-Broadway and played to critical acclaim into the summer. In the spring of 1969 it toured the United States, under the unique sponsorship of the Goethe Institute in Munich, playing on college campuses from coast to coast. Willson's translation of *The Wicked Cooks* (Die bösen Köche) was produced off-Broadway in January, 1967, and published in *Four Plays* the same year. For the occasion of the Grass Symposium in April, 1970, at The University of Texas at Austin, Willson translated *Uptight* (Davor), which was premiered in English in six performances.

ANDRZEJ WIRTH was born and reared in Poland, where he took part in the Warsaw Uprising of 1944. In 1947 Wirth began his study of philosophy, concentrating on aesthetics, at the University of Lódz and then Warsaw, where he received the M.A. in aesthetics in 1951. He received the Ph.D. degree from the University of Breslau (Wroclaw) in 1965, writing a dissertation on the stereometric structure of the plays of Bertolt Brecht (published both in Germany and in Poland). Because of his distinguished work on Brecht and his interest in theater, he was invited by Brecht to Berlin in 1956 to work with the Ensemble. He has been a member of the Group 47 since 1958, mediating effectively between the literatures of Eastern and Western Europe. Both in his capacity as editor of *Polityka* and *Nowa Kultura* and through his own translations he introduced a number of German authors to Polish readers. Wirth first drew attention to the innovative and impressive dramaturgy of Jerzy Grotowski, who during the past ten years has won renown internationally. In 1966 Wirth attended the Princeton meeting of the Group 47 and then remained in the United States as a guest professor at the University of Massachusetts at Amherst and at Stanford University. He is presently on the faculty of the Department of Theater in Lehmann College at the City University of New York.

INDEX OF NAMES AND TITLES

Adamov, Arthur: 63
"Advent": 77, 82–83
Adventures of Augie March, The (Bellow): 57
Ahnen, Die. SEE *The Forebears*
Akzente (magazine): 68
Animal Farm (Orwell): 64
Arp, Hans: 73, 78
"Askese." SEE "Askesis"
"Askesis": 61
Ausgefragt: 9, 12–13, 78, 80, 82, 83
"Ausverkauf." SEE "Sale"

Baden-Baden Didactic Play of Acquiescence, The (Brecht): 21
Badener Lehrstück vom Einverständnis, Das. SEE *The Baden-Baden Didactic Play of Acquiescence*
Bald Soprano, The (Ionesco): 64
Ballerina, The: 16–17
Barthel, Kuba: 23
Beckett, Samuel: 64, 66
Bellow, Saul: 48, 57, 58, 59
Benn, Gottfried: 71
Beritten hin und zurück. SEE *Rocking Back and Forth*
Biermann, Wolf: 85
Blechtrommel, Die. SEE *The Tin Drum*
bösen Köche, Die. SEE *The Wicked Cooks*
"bösen Schuhe, Die." SEE "The Wicked Shoes"
Brecht, Bertolt: 18–31, 65, 68, 71, 72, 78, 82, 84
"Brief über den Roman" (F. Schlegel): 49
"Buckower Elegien" (Brecht): 78
Bultmann, Rudolf: 60

Čapek, Karel: 64
Cat and Mouse: 34, 35, 62, 64, 73
Caves du Vatican (Gide). SEE *Lafcadio's Adventures*
"Chain Smoking": 9
Chairs, The (Ionesco): 63
Churchill, Winston: 19
Cocteau, Jean: 66
"Content as Resistance": 4–5, 71
Coriolan (Brecht): 18, 25
Coriolanus (Shakespeare): 18, 23, 24, 25, 69

"Dampfkessel-Effekt, Der." SEE "The Steam Boiler Effect"
Davor. SEE *Uptight*
Days of the Commune, The (Brecht): 20
Defoe, Daniel: 50
Demian (Hesse): 55
Deputy, The (Hochhuth): 18, 25, 28, 60
Deutsche Literatur in West und Ost (Reich-Ranicki): 49
"Diana—or the Objects": 7

Diderot, Denis: 53
Döblin, Alfred: 57
Dog Years: 32, 34, 46, 49, 58, 60, 61, 62, 63, 64
Doktor Faustus (T. Mann): 53
"Do Something": 9–11, 82
Dream and Derangement (Trakl): 56
"Drehorgeln kurz vor Ostern": 69
"Drei Wochen Später." SEE "Three Weeks Later"
Dubček, Alexander: 21

Edschmid, Kasimir: 56
"Ehe." SEE "Marriage"
Engel, Erich: 23
Enzensberger, Hans Magnus: 85
Ermittlung, Die (Weiss). SEE *The Investigation*
Esslin, Martin: 62, 64, 67

Fallada, Hans: 61
"Falsche Schönheit." SEE "Wrong Beauty"
"Familiär." SEE "Family Matters"
"Family Matters": 77–78
Faulkner, William: 55
Faust (Goethe): 65
Flood: 8, 26, 64, 66
"Flood": 8
Fontane, Theodor: 61, 67
Forebears, The (Freytag): 53
Freytag, Gustav: 53

Gide, André: 55
Gitter, Dean: 24
Glasperlenspiel, Das (Hesse). SEE *The Glass-Bead Game*
Glass-Bead Game, The (Hesse): 55
Gleisdreieck: 7, 8, 9, 61, 78, 79
Goethe, Johann Wolfgang: 55, 56, 64, 65
Golding, William: 59
Goldmann, Lucien: 35
Graves, Robert: 70
Günter Grass (Kurt Lothar Tank): 5

Hammarskjold, Dag: 19
Hatfield, Henry: 64
heilige Johanna der Schlachthöfe, Die (Brecht). SEE *Saint Joan of the Stockyards*
Hesse, Hermann: 55
Hochhuth, Rolf: 18, 19, 24, 25, 28, 31, 60
Hochwasser. SEE *Flood*
"Hochwasser." SEE "Flood"
Hundejahre. SEE *Dog Years*

"Im Ei." SEE "In the Egg"
Immoralist, The (Gide): 55

In der Sache J. Robert Oppenheimer. SEE *In the Matter of J. Robert Oppen-heimer*
"Inhalt als Widerstand, Der." SEE "Content as Resistance"
"In Ohnmacht gefallen." SEE "Powerless, with a Guitar"
"In the Egg": 79
In the Matter of J. Robert Oppenheimer (Kipphardt): 25
Investigation, The (Weiss): 19, 25
Ionesco, Eugène: 63, 64
"Irgendwas machen." SEE "Do Something"
"Ironic Landscape" (Klabund): 57

"Jellied Pig's Head, The": 82
"John Maynard" (Fontane): 67

Kafka, Franz: 48
Kahler, Erich: 56
Kaschnitz, Marie Luise: 69
Katz und Maus. SEE *Cat and Mouse*
Kesting, Marianne: 68
"Kinderlied": 79–80
Kipphardt, Heinar: 18, 25
Klabund (Alfred Henschke): 57
"Kleckerburg": 69, 73, 82
Kolakowski, Leszek: 21
Kunze, Reiner: 85
Kuron, Jacek: 21

Lafcadio's Adventures (Gide): 55
Le nouveau locataire (Ionesco). SEE *The New Tenant*
Le ping-pong (Adamov): 63
Les chaises (Ionesco). SEE *The Chairs*
Lewis, R. W. B.: 59
Life of Edward II of England, The (Marlowe): 25
L'Immoraliste (Gide). SEE *The Immoralist*
Lindenberger, Herbert: 19
Local Anaesthetic: 10, 32–45, 62, 63, 64, 65, 69, 70

Mann, Thomas: 48, 53
Marlowe, Christopher: 25
"Marriage": 83
Marxist Studies (Brecht): 27
Mayer, Timothy Swayze: 24
Me-ti, Book of Changes (Brecht): 29
Me-ti, Buch der Wendungen (Brecht). SEE *Me-ti, Book of Changes*
Mister, Mister: 66
Modzelewski, Karol: 21
Moore, Marianne: 46
"Musik im Freien." SEE "Open Air Concert"
Myasnikov, Alexander: 33

Napoleon: 60
New Tenant, The (Ionesco): 63
Noch zehn Minuten bis Buffalo. SEE *Only Ten Minutes to Buffalo*

"Of the Residue under Our Nails": 83
Onkel, Onkel. SEE *Mister, Mister*
Only Ten Minutes to Buffalo: 5, 26, 67, 68
"On the Lack of Self-confidence among Writing Court Fools in View of Non-existent Courts": 4n., 32n., 72
"Open Air Concert": 69
Oppenheimer, J. Robert: 18, 19, 25
Orphée (Cocteau): 66
örtlich betäubt. SEE *Local Anaesthetic*
Orwell, George: 64

Pirandello, Luigi: 66
Pius XII: 19, 25
Plebeians Rehearse the Uprising, The: 18–19, 23–31, 33, 65, 66, 68
Plebejer proben den Aufstand, Die. SEE *The Plebeians Rehearse the Uprising*
"Powerless, with a Guitar": 80–82
"Prehistory and Posthistory of the Tragedy of Coriolanus from Livy and Plutarch via Shakespeare to Brecht and Myself, The": 25
Princeton Lecture of 1966. SEE "On the Lack of Self-confidence among Writing Court Fools in View of Non-existent Courts"

Raabe, Wilhelm: 61
Raleigh, Sir Walter: 24
Reich-Ranicki, Marcel: 49, 50
Rocking Back and Forth: 60, 65, 66
Rousseau, Jean Jacques: 53
Rühmkorf, Peter: 85

Saint Joan of the Stockyards (Brecht): 20–21
"Sale": 78–79
"Saturn": 79
"Scarecrows, The": 69
"Scheinekopfsülze, Die." SEE "The Jellied Pig's Head"
Schiller, Friedrich: 19, 31, 32
Schlegel, Friedrich: 49, 50, 59, 62
"School for Tenors, The": 74–77
"Schule der Tenöre, Die." SEE "The School for Tenors"
"Sea Battle, The": 8
Shakespeare, William: 18, 24, 25, 26, 27, 28, 29, 30, 50, 68, 69
Stalin, Joseph: 24, 26
"Steam Boiler Effect, The": 82
Stellvertreter, Der (Hochhuth). SEE *The Deputy*
Sterne, Laurence: 53
Swift, Jonathan: 64

Tage der Kommune, Die (Brecht). SEE *The Days of the Commune*
Tank, Kurt Lothar: 5
Thirty-two Teeth: 68
"Three Weeks Later": 9
Tin Drum, The: 8, 34, 46–59, 60, 62, 63, 64, 65, 73, 77, 78
Tolstoy, Leo: 60
Trakl, Georg: 56

Traum und Umnachtung (Trakl). SEE *Dream and Derangement*

Uptight: 9, 26, 33, 35, 40, 62, 64, 69, 70
Utzerath, Hansjörg: 23

"Vermont": 12–13
"Vogelscheuchen, Die." SEE "The Scarecrows"
"Vom mangelnden Selbstvertrauen der schreibenden Hofnarren unter Berücksichtigung nicht vorhandener Höfe." SEE "On the Lack of Self-confidence among Writing Court Fools in View of Non-existent Courts"
"Vom Rest unterm Nagel." SEE "Of the Residue under Our Nails"
"Vor- und Nachgeschichte der Tragödie des Coriolanus von Livius und Plutarch über Shakespeare bis zu Brecht und mir." SEE "The Prehistory and Posthistory of the Tragedy of Coriolanus from Livy and Plutarch via Shakespeare to Brecht and Myself"
Vorzüge der Windhühner, Die: 8, 71, 73, 78

Waiting for Godot (Beckett): 64
War and Peace (Tolstoy): 60
"Was ist des Deutschen Vaterland?" (campaign speech). SEE "What is the German Fatherland?"
Weigel, Helene: 23
Weiss, Peter: 18–19, 24
"What is the German Fatherland?" (campaign speech): 21
Wicked Cooks, The: 26, 67
"Wicked Shoes, The": 13–15
Wilhelm Meister (Goethe): 48
"Wrong Beauty": 83–84

Zweiunddreißig Zähne. SEE *Thirty-two Teeth*